MW00807441

ORDER OF
CHRISTIAN FUNERALS:
RITE OF COMMITTAL

THE ROMAN RITUAL

REVISED BY DECREE OF THE
SECOND VATICAN ECUMENICAL
COUNCIL AND PUBLISHED BY
AUTHORITY OF POPE PAUL VI

LITURGY TRAINING PUBLICATIONS
CHICAGO   1989

ORDER OF CHRISTIAN FUNERALS

APPROVED FOR USE IN THE DIOCESES OF THE UNITED STATES OF AMERICA BY THE NATIONAL CONFERENCE OF CATHOLIC BISHOPS AND CONFIRMED BY THE APOSTOLIC SEE

RITE OF COMMITTAL

Prepared by
International Commission on English in the Liturgy
A Joint Commission of Catholic Bishops' Conferences

Concordat cum originali: Ronald F. Krisman, Executive Director
Secretariat for the Liturgy
National Conference of Catholic Bishops

Approved by the National Conference of Catholic Bishops for use in the dioceses of the United States of America, 14 November 1985. Confirmed by decree of the Congregation for Divine Worship, 29 April 1987 (Prot. N. CD 1550/85).

Published by authority of the Committee on the Liturgy, National Conference of Catholic Bishops.

ACKNOWLEDGMENTS

The English translation, original texts, general introduction, pastoral notes, arrangement, and design of *Order of Christian Funerals* © 1989, 1985, International Committee on English in the Liturgy, Inc. (ICEL); excerpts from the English translation of *The Roman Missal* © 1973, ICEL.

The Scripture readings are taken from *The New American Bible with Revised New Testament*, copyright © 1986, Confraternity of Christian Doctrine, Washington D.C. Used by license of copyright owner. All rights reserved.

Prayer texts of committal, "In sure and certain hope . . ." and "Into your hands, O merciful Savior, . . .," used by permission, from the *Book of Common Prayer*, 1979, published by The Church Pension Fund.

ISBN 0-929650-13-1

Cover art, Steve Erspamer.

Printed and bound in the United States of America.

Copyright © 1989, Archdiocese of Chicago. All rights reserved.

Liturgy Training Publications, 1800 North Hermitage Avenue, Chicago, Illinois 60622-1101; 312/486-7008.

NATIONAL CONFERENCE OF CATHOLIC BISHOPS

UNITED STATES OF AMERICA

DECREE

In accord with the norms established by decree of the Sacred Congregation of Rites *Cum, nostra aetate* (27 January 1966), the *Order of Christian Funerals* is declared to be the vernacular typical edition of the *Ordo Exsequiarum* for the dioceses of the United States of America, and may be published by authority of the National Conference of Catholic Bishops.

The *Order of Christian Funerals* was canonically approved by the National Conference of Catholic Bishops in plenary assembly on 14 November 1985 and was subsequently confirmed by the Apostolic See by decree of the Congregation for Divine Worship on 29 April 1987 (Prot. N. CD 1550/85).

On 1 October 1989 the *Order of Christian Funerals* may be published and used in funeral celebrations. From All Souls Day, 2 November 1989, its use is mandatory in the dioceses of the United States of America. From that date forward no other English version of these rites may be used.

Given at the General Secretariat of the National Conference of Catholic Bishops, Washington, D.C., on 15 August 1989, the Solemnity of the Assumption.

✠ John L. May
Archbishop of Saint Louis
President
National Conference of Catholic Bishops

Robert N. Lynch
General Secretary

CONTENTS

EDITORIAL NOTE

Beginning with the General Introduction, the numbering system in this book diverges from the Latin edition of *Ordo Exsequiarum*. The new numbering system appears at the left-hand side of the page. The corresponding number from the Latin edition appears in the right-hand margin. A text having a number on the left but no reference number in the right-hand margin is either newly composed or is a text from *The Roman Missal, Holy Communion and Worship of the Eucharist outside Mass, The Liturgy of the Hours,* or *Pastoral Care of the Sick: Rites of Anointing and Viaticum.*

All of the numbers used in this volume, *Rite of Committal,* correspond to the numbers in the *Order of Christian Funerals.*

"Funeral rites" is a general designation used of all the liturgical celebrations in the *Order of Christian Funerals.* "Funeral liturgy" is a more particular designation applied to the two forms of liturgical celebration presented under the headings "Funeral Mass" and "Funeral Liturgy outside Mass."

CONGREGATION FOR DIVINE WORSHIP

Prot. no. 720/69

DECREE

By means of the funeral rites it has been the practice of the Church, as a tender mother, not simply to commend the dead to God but also to raise high the hope of its children and to give witness to its own faith in the future resurrection of the baptized with Christ.

Vatican Council II accordingly directed in the Constitution on the Liturgy that the funeral rites be revised in such a way that they would more clearly express the paschal character of the Christian's death and also that the rites for the burial of children would have a proper Mass (art. 81-82).

The Consilium prepared the desired rites and put them into trial use in different parts of the world. Now Pope Paul VI by his apostolic authority has approved and ordered the publication of these rites as henceforth obligatory for all those using the Roman Ritual.

Also by order of Pope Paul this Congregation for Divine Worship promulgates the *Order of Funerals*, stipulating that its effective date is 1 June 1970.

The Congregation further establishes that until 1 June 1970, when Latin is used in celebrating funerals there is an option to use either the present rite or the rite now in the Roman Ritual; after 1 June 1970 only this new *Order of Funerals* is to be used.

Once the individual conferences of bishops have prepared a vernacular version of the rite and received its confirmation from this Congregation, they have authorization to fix any other, feasible effective date prior to 1 June 1970 for use of the *Order of Funerals*.

All things to the contrary notwithstanding.

Congregation for Divine Worship, 15 August 1969, the solemnity of the Assumption.

Benno Cardinal Gut
Prefect

A. Bugnini
Secretary

Say of Funerals
70c

ORDER OF
CHRISTIAN FUNERALS

Why do you search for the Living One among the dead?

ORDER OF CHRISTIAN FUNERALS

GENERAL INTRODUCTION

1   In the face of death, the Church confidently proclaims that God has created each person for eternal life and that Jesus, the Son of God, by his death and resurrection, has broken the chains of sin and death that bound humanity. Christ "achieved his task of redeeming humanity and giving perfect glory to God, principally by the paschal mystery of his blessed passion, resurrection from the dead, and glorious ascension."[1]

2   The proclamation of Jesus Christ "who was put to death for our sins and raised to life to justify us" (Romans 4:25) is at the center of the Church's life. The mystery of the Lord's death and resurrection gives power to all of the Church's activity. "For it was from the side of Christ as he slept the sleep of death upon the cross that there came forth the sublime sacrament of the whole Church."[2] The Church's liturgical and sacramental life and proclamation of the Gospel make this mystery present in the life of the faithful. Through the sacraments of baptism, confirmation, and eucharist, men and women are initiated into this mystery. "You have been taught that when we were baptized in Christ Jesus we were baptized into his death; in other words when we were baptized we went into the tomb with him and joined him in death, so that as Christ was raised from the dead by the Father's glory, we too might live a new life. If in union with Christ we have imitated his death, we shall also imitate him in his resurrection" (Romans 6:3-5).

3   In the eucharistic sacrifice, the Church's celebration of Christ's Passover from death to life, the faith of the baptized in the paschal mystery is renewed and nourished. Their union with Christ and with each other is strengthened: "Because there is one bread, we who are many, are one body, for we all partake of the one bread" (1 Corinthians 10:17).

4   At the death of a Christian, whose life of faith was begun in the waters of baptism and strengthened at the eucharistic table, the Church intercedes on behalf of the deceased because of its confident belief that death is not the end nor does it break the bonds forged in life. The Church also ministers to the sorrowing and consoles them in the funeral rites with the comforting word of God and the sacrament of the eucharist.

---

[1] Vatican Council II, Constitution on the Liturgy *Sacrosanctum Concilium*, art. 5.

[2] Ibid.

5   Christians celebrate the funeral rites to offer worship, praise, and thanksgiving to God for the gift of a life which has now been returned to God, the author of life and the hope of the just. The Mass, the memorial of Christ's death and resurrection, is the principal celebration of the Christian funeral.

6   The Church through its funeral rites commends the dead to God's merciful love and pleads for the forgiveness of their sins. At the funeral rites, especially at the celebration of the eucharistic sacrifice, the Christian community affirms and expresses the union of the Church on earth with the Church in heaven in the one great communion of saints. Though separated from the living, the dead are still at one with the community of believers on earth and benefit from their prayers and intercession. At the rite of final commendation and farewell, the community acknowledges the reality of separation and commends the deceased to God. In this way it recognizes the spiritual bond that still exists between the living and the dead and proclaims its belief that all the faithful will be raised up and reunited in the new heavens and a new earth, where death will be no more.

7   The celebration of the Christian funeral brings hope and consolation to the living. While proclaiming the Gospel of Jesus Christ and witnessing to Christian hope in the resurrection, the funeral rites also recall to all who take part in them God's mercy and judgment and meet the human need to turn always to God in times of crisis.

MINISTRY AND PARTICIPATION

8   "If one member suffers in the body of Christ which is the Church, all the members suffer with that member" (1 Corinthians 12:26). For this reason, those who are baptized into Christ and nourished at the same table of the Lord are responsible for one another. When Christians are sick, their brothers and sisters share a ministry of mutual charity and "do all that they can to help the sick return to health, by showing love for the sick, and by celebrating the sacraments with them."[3] So too when a member of Christ's Body dies, the faithful are called to a ministry of consolation to those who have suffered the loss of one whom they love. Christian consolation is rooted in that hope that comes from faith in the saving death and resurrection of the Lord Jesus Christ. Christian hope faces the reality of death and the anguish of grief but trusts confidently that the power of sin and death has been vanquished by the risen Lord. The Church calls each member of Christ's Body—priest, deacon, layperson—to participate

---

[3] See Roman Ritual, *Pastoral Care of the Sick: Rites of Anointing and Viaticum*, General Introduction, no. 33.

in the ministry of consolation: to care for the dying, to pray for the dead, to comfort those who mourn.

COMMUNITY

9   The responsibility for the ministry of consolation rests with the believing community, which heeds the words and example of the Lord Jesus: "Blessed are they who mourn; they shall be consoled" (Matthew 5:3). Each Christian shares in this ministry according to the various gifts and offices in the Church. As part of the pastoral ministry, pastors, associate pastors, and other ministers should instruct the parish community on the Christian meaning of death and on the purpose and significance of the Church's liturgical rites for the dead. Information on how the parish community assists families in preparing for funerals should also be provided.

By giving instruction, pastors and associate pastors should lead the community to a deeper appreciation of its role in the ministry of consolation and to a fuller understanding of the significance of the death of a fellow Christian. Often the community must respond to the anguish voiced by Martha, the sister of Lazarus: "Lord, if you had been here, my brother would never have died" (John 11:21) and must console those who mourn, as Jesus himself consoled Martha: "Your brother will rise again. . . . I am the resurrection and the life: those who believe in me, though they should die, will come to life; and those who are alive and believe in me will never die" (John 11:25-26). The faith of the Christian community in the resurrection of the dead brings support and strength to those who suffer the loss of those whom they love.

10   Members of the community should console the mourners with words of faith and support and with acts of kindness, for example, assisting them with some of the routine tasks of daily living. Such assistance may allow members of the family to devote time to planning the funeral rites with the priest and other ministers and may also give the family time for prayer and mutual comfort.

11   The community's principal involvement in the ministry of consolation is expressed in its active participation in the celebration of the funeral rites, particularly the vigil for the deceased, the funeral liturgy, and the rite of committal. For this reason these rites should be scheduled at times that permit as many of the community as possible to be present. The assembly's participation can be assisted by the preparation of booklets that contain an outline of the rite, the texts and songs belonging to the people, and directions for posture, gesture, and movement.

12   At the vigil for the deceased or on another occasion before the eucharistic celebration, the presiding minister should invite all to be present at the funeral liturgy and to take an active part in it. The minister may

also describe the funeral liturgy and explain why the community gathers to hear the word of God proclaimed and to celebrate the eucharist when one of the faithful dies.

Pastors, associate pastors, and other ministers should also be mindful of those persons who are not members of the Catholic Church, or Catholics who are not involved in the life of the Church.

13   As a minister of reconciliation, the priest should be especially sensitive to the possible needs for reconciliation felt by the family and others. Funerals can begin the process of reconciling differences and supporting those ties that can help the bereaved adjust to the loss brought about by death. With attentiveness to each situation, the priest can help to begin the process of reconciliation when needed. In some cases this process may find expression in the celebration of the sacrament of penance, either before the funeral liturgy or at a later time.

LITURGICAL MINISTERS

Presiding Minister

14   Priests, as teachers of faith and ministers of comfort, preside at the funeral rites, especially the Mass; the celebration of the funeral liturgy is especially entrusted to pastors and associate pastors. When no priest is available, deacons, as ministers of the word, of the altar, and of charity, preside at funeral rites. When no priest or deacon is available for the vigil and related rites or the rite of committal, a layperson presides.

Other Liturgical Ministers

15   In the celebration of the funeral rites laymen and laywomen may serve as readers, musicians, ushers, pallbearers, and, according to existing norms, as special ministers of the eucharist. Pastors and other priests should instill in these ministers an appreciation of how much the reverent exercise of their ministries contributes to the celebration of the funeral rites. Family members should be encouraged to take an active part in these ministries, but they should not be asked to assume any role that their grief or sense of loss may make too burdensome.

MINISTRY FOR THE MOURNERS AND THE DECEASED

FAMILY AND FRIENDS

16   In planning and carrying out the funeral rites the pastor and all other ministers should keep in mind the life of the deceased and the circumstances of death. They should also take into consideration the spiritual and psychological needs of the family and friends of the deceased to express grief

and their sense of loss, to accept the reality of death, and to comfort one another.

17   Whenever possible, ministers should involve the family in planning the funeral rites: in the choice of texts and rites provided in the ritual, in the selection of music for the rites, and in the designation of liturgical ministers.

Planning of the funeral rites may take place during the visit of the pastor or other minister at some appropriate time after the death and before the vigil service. Ministers should explain to the family the meaning and significance of each of the funeral rites, especially the vigil, the funeral liturgy, and the rite of committal.

If pastoral and personal considerations allow, the period before death may be an appropriate time to plan the funeral rites with the family and even with the family member who is dying. Although planning the funeral before death should be approached with sensitivity and care, it can have the effect of helping the one who is dying and the family face the reality of death with Christian hope. It can also help relieve the family of numerous details after the death and may allow them to benefit more fully from the celebration of the funeral rites.

DECEASED

18   Through the celebration of the funeral rites, the Church manifests its care for the dead, both baptized members and catechumens. In keeping with the provisions of *Codex Iuris Canonici*, can. 1183, the Church's funeral rites may be celebrated for a child who died before baptism and whose parents intended to have the child baptized.

At the discretion of the local Ordinary, the Church's funeral rites may be celebrated for a baptized member of another Church or ecclesial community provided this would not be contrary to the wishes of the deceased person and provided the minister of the Church or ecclesial community in which the deceased person was a regular member or communicant is unavailable.

19   Since in baptism the body was marked with the seal of the Trinity and became the temple of the Holy Spirit, Christians respect and honor the bodies of the dead and the places where they rest. Any customs associated with the preparation of the body of the deceased should always be marked with dignity and reverence and never with the despair of those who have no hope. Preparation of the body should include prayer, especially at those intimate moments reserved for family members. For the final disposition of the body, it is the ancient Christian custom to bury or entomb the bodies of the dead; cremation is permitted, unless it is evident that cremation was chosen for anti-Christian motives.

20   In countries or regions where an undertaker, and not the family or community, carries out the preparation and transfer of the body, the

pastor and other ministers are to ensure that the undertakers appreciate the values and beliefs of the Christian community.

The family and friends of the deceased should not be excluded from taking part in the services sometimes provided by undertakers, for example, the preparation and laying out of the body.

LITURGICAL ELEMENTS

21   Since liturgical celebration involves the whole person, it requires attentiveness to all that affects the senses. The readings and prayers, psalms and songs should be proclaimed or sung with understanding, conviction, and reverence. Music for the assembly should be truly expressive of the texts and at the same time simple and easily sung. The ritual gestures, processions, and postures should express and foster an attitude of reverence and reflectiveness in those taking part in the funeral rites. The funeral rites should be celebrated in an atmosphere of simple beauty, in a setting that encourages participation. Liturgical signs and symbols affirming Christian belief and hope in the paschal mystery are abundant in the celebration of the funeral rites, but their undue multiplication or repetition should be avoided. Care must be taken that the choice and use of signs and symbols are in accord with the culture of the people.

THE WORD OF GOD

Readings

22   In every celebration for the dead, the Church attaches great importance to the reading of the word of God. The readings proclaim to the assembly the paschal mystery, teach remembrance of the dead, convey the hope of being gathered together again in God's kingdom, and encourage the witness of Christian life. Above all, the readings tell of God's designs for a world in which suffering and death will relinquish their hold on all whom God has called his own. A careful selection and use of readings from Scripture for the funeral rites will provide the family and the community with an opportunity to hear God speak to them in their needs, sorrows, fears, and hopes.

23   In the celebration of the liturgy of the word at the funeral liturgy, the biblical readings may not be replaced by nonbiblical readings. But during prayer services with the family nonbiblical readings may be used in addition to readings from Scripture.

24   Liturgical tradition assigns the proclamation of the readings in the celebration of the liturgy of the word to readers and the deacon. The presiding minister proclaims the readings only when there are no assisting

ministers present. Those designated to proclaim the word of God should prepare themselves to exercise this ministry.[5]

Psalmody

25   The psalms are rich in imagery, feeling, and symbolism. They power-fully express the suffering and pain, the hope and trust of people of every age and culture. Above all the psalms sing of faith in God, of revelation and redemption. They enable the assembly to pray in the words that Jesus himself used during his life on earth. Jesus, who knew anguish and the fear of death, "offered up prayer and entreaty, aloud and in silent tears, to the one who had the power to save him out of death. . . . Although he was Son, he learned to obey through suffering; but having been made per-fect, he became for all who obey him the source of eternal salvation . . ." (Hebrews 5:7-9). In the psalms the members of the assembly pray in the voice of Christ, who intercedes on their behalf before the Father.[6] The Church, like Christ, turns again and again to the psalms as a genuine ex-pression of grief and of praise and as a sure source of trust and hope in times of trial. Pastors and other ministers are, therefore, to make an ear-nest effort through an effective catechesis to lead their communities to a clearer and deeper grasp of at least some of the psalms provided for the funeral rites.

26   The psalms are designated for use in many places in the funeral rites (for example, as responses to the readings, for the processions, for use at the vigil for the deceased). Since the psalms are songs, whenever possible, they should be sung.

Homily

27   A brief homily based on the readings is always given after the gospel reading at the funeral liturgy and may also be given after the readings at the vigil service; but there is never to be a eulogy. Attentive to the grief of those present, the homilist should dwell on God's compassionate love and on the paschal mystery of the Lord, as proclaimed in the Scripture readings. The homilist should also help the members of the assembly to understand that the mystery of God's love and the mystery of Jesus' vic-torious death and resurrection were present in the life and death of the deceased and that these mysteries are active in their own lives as well. Through the homily members of the family and community should re-ceive consolation and strength to face the death of one of their members with a hope nourished by the saving word of God. Laypersons who pre-side at the funeral rites give an instruction on the readings.

---

[5] See *Lectionary for Mass* (2nd *editio typica*, 1981), General Introduction, nos. 49, 52, and 55.

[6] See General Instruction of the Liturgy of the Hours, no. 109.

PRAYERS AND INTERCESSIONS

28 In the presidential prayers of the funeral rites the presiding minister addresses God on behalf of the deceased and the mourners in the name of the entire Church. From the variety of prayers provided the minister in consultation with the family should carefully select texts that truly capture the unspoken prayers and hopes of the assembly and also respond to the needs of the mourners.

29 Having heard the word of God proclaimed and preached, the assembly responds at the vigil and at the funeral liturgy with prayers of intercession for the deceased and all the dead, for the family and all who mourn, and for all in the assembly. The holy people of God, confident in their belief in the communion of saints, exercise their royal priesthood by joining together in this prayer for all those who have died.[7]

Several models of intercessions are provided within the rites for adaptation to the circumstances.

MUSIC

30 Music is integral to the funeral rites. It allows the community to express convictions and feelings that words alone may fail to convey. It has the power to console and uplift the mourners and to strengthen the unity of the assembly in faith and love. The texts of the songs chosen for a particular celebration should express the paschal mystery of the Lord's suffering, death, and triumph over death and should be related to the readings from Scripture.

31 Since music can evoke strong feelings, the music for the celebration of the funeral rites should be chosen with great care. The music at funerals should support, console, and uplift the participants and should help to create in them a spirit of hope in Christ's victory over death and in the Christian's share in that victory.

32 Music should be provided for the vigil and funeral liturgy and, whenever possible, for the funeral processions and the rite of committal. The specific notes that precede each of these rites suggest places in the rites where music is appropriate. Many musical settings used by the parish community during the liturgical year may be suitable for use at funerals. Efforts should be made to develop and expand the parish's repertoire for use at funerals.

33 An organist or other instrumentalist, a cantor, and, whenever possible, even a choir should assist the assembly's full participation in singing the songs, responses, and acclamations of these rites.

---

[7] See *De Oratione communi seu fidelium* (2nd ed., Vatican Polyglot Press, 1966), chapter 1, no. 3, p. 7: tr., *Documents on the Liturgy* (The Liturgical Press, 1982), no. 1893.

SILENCE

34   Prayerful silence is an element important to the celebration of the funeral rites. Intervals of silence should be observed, for example, after each reading and during the final commendation and farewell, to permit the assembly to reflect upon the word of God and the meaning of the celebration.

SYMBOLS

Easter Candle and Other Candles

35   The Easter candle reminds the faithful of Christ's undying presence among them, of his victory over sin and death, and of their share in that victory by virtue of their initiation. It recalls the Easter Vigil, the night when the Church awaits the Lord's resurrection and when new light for the living and the dead is kindled. During the funeral liturgy and also during the vigil service, when celebrated in the church, the Easter candle may be placed beforehand near the position the coffin will occupy at the conclusion of the procession.

   According to local custom, other candles may also be placed near the coffin during the funeral liturgy as a sign of reverence and solemnity.

Holy Water

36   Blessed or holy water reminds the assembly of the saving waters of baptism. In the rite of reception of the body at the church, its use calls to mind the deceased's baptism and initiation into the community of faith. In the rite of final commendation the gesture of sprinkling may also signify farewell.

Incense

37   Incense is used during the funeral rites as a sign of honor to the body of the deceased, which through baptism became the temple of the Holy Spirit. Incense is also used as a sign of the community's prayers for the deceased rising to the throne of God and as a sign of farewell.

Other Symbols

38   If it is the custom in the local community, a pall may be placed over the coffin when it is received at the church. A reminder of the baptismal garment of the deceased, the pall is a sign of the Christian dignity of the person. The use of the pall also signifies that all are equal in the eyes of God (see James 2:1-9).

   A Book of the Gospels or a Bible may be placed on the coffin as a sign that Christians live by the word of God and that fidelity to that word leads to eternal life.

A cross may be placed on the coffin as a reminder that the Christian is marked by the cross in baptism and through Jesus' suffering on the cross is brought to the victory of his resurrection.

Fresh flowers, used in moderation, can enhance the setting of the funeral rites.

Only Christian symbols may rest on or be placed near the coffin during the funeral liturgy. Any other symbols, for example, national flags, or flags or insignia of associations, have no place in the funeral liturgy (see no. 132).

Liturgical Color

39   The liturgical color chosen for funerals should express Christian hope but should not be offensive to human grief or sorrow. In the United States, white, violet, or black vestments may be worn at the funeral rites and at other offices and Masses for the dead.

RITUAL GESTURES AND MOVEMENT

40   The presiding minister or an assisting minister may quietly direct the assembly in the movements, gestures, and posture appropriate to the particular ritual moment or action.

41   Processions, especially when accompanied with music and singing, can strengthen the bond of communion in the assembly. For processions, ministers of music should give preference to settings of psalms and songs that are responsorial or litanic in style and that allow the people to respond to the verses with an invariable refrain. During the various processions, it is preferable that the pallbearers carry the coffin as a sign of reverence and respect for the deceased.

42   Processions continue to have special significance in funeral celebrations, as in Christian Rome where funeral rites consisted of three "stages" or "stations" joined by two processions. Christians accompanied the body on its last journey. From the home of the deceased the Christian community proceeded to the church singing psalms. When the service in the church concluded, the body was carried in solemn procession to the grave or tomb. During the final procession the congregation sang psalms praising the God of mercy and redemption and antiphons entrusting the deceased to the care of the angels and saints. The funeral liturgy mirrored the journey of human life, the Christian pilgrimage to the heavenly Jerusalem.

In many places and situations a solemn procession on foot to the church or to the place of committal may not be possible. Nevertheless at the conclusion of the funeral liturgy an antiphon or versicle and response may be sung as the body is taken to the entrance of the church. Psalms, hymns, or liturgical songs may also be sung when the participants gather at the place of committal.

SELECTION OF RITES FROM
THE ORDER OF CHRISTIAN FUNERALS

43 The *Order of Christian Funerals* makes provision for the minister, in consultation with the family, to choose those rites and texts that are most suitable to the situation: those that most closely apply to the needs of the mourners, the circumstances of the death, and the customs of the local Christian community. The minister and family may be assisted in the choice of a rite or rites by the reflections preceding each rite or group of rites.

44 Part I, "Funeral Rites," of the *Order of Christian Funerals* provides those rites that may be used in the funerals of Christians and is divided into three groups of rites that correspond in general to the three principal ritual moments in Christian funerals: "Vigil and Related Rites and Prayers," "Funeral Liturgy," and "Rite of Committal."

45 The section entitled "Vigil and Related Rites and Prayers" includes rites that may be celebrated between the time of death and the funeral liturgy or, should there be no funeral liturgy, before the rite of committal. The vigil is the principal celebration of the Christian community during the time before the funeral liturgy. It may take the form of a liturgy of the word (see nos. 54-97) or of some part of the office for the dead (see Part IV, nos. 348-395). Two vigil services are provided: "Vigil for the Deceased" and "Vigil for the Deceased with Reception at the Church." The second service is used when the vigil is celebrated in the church and the body is to be received at this time.

"Related Rites and Prayers" includes three brief rites that may be used on occasions of prayer with the family: "Prayers after Death," "Gathering in the Presence of the Body," and "Transfer of the Body to the Church or to the Place of Committal." These rites are examples or models of what can be done and should be adapted to the circumstances.

46 The section entitled "Funeral Liturgy" provides two forms of the funeral liturgy, the central celebration of the Christian community for the deceased: "Funeral Mass" and "Funeral Liturgy outside Mass." When one of its members dies, the Church especially encourages the celebration of the Mass. When Mass cannot be celebrated (see no. 178), the second form of the funeral liturgy may be used and a Mass for the deceased should be celebrated, if possible, at a later time.

47 The section entitled "Rite of Committal" includes two forms of the rite of committal, the concluding rite of the funeral: "Rite of Committal"

and "Rite of Committal with Final Commendation." The first form is used when the final commendation is celebrated as part of the conclusion of the funeral liturgy. The second form is used when the final commendation does not take place during the funeral liturgy or when no funeral liturgy precedes the committal.

48   Part II, "Funeral Rites for Children," provides an adaptation of the principal rites in Part I: "Vigil for a Deceased Child," "Funeral Liturgy," and "Rite of Committal." These rites may be used in the funerals of infants and young children, including those of early school age. The rites in Part II include texts for use in the case of a baptized child and in the case of a child who died before baptism.

In some instances, for example, the death of an infant, the vigil and funeral liturgy may not be appropriate. Only the rite of committal and perhaps one of the forms of prayer with the family as provided in "Related Rites and Prayers" may be desirable. Part II does not contain "Related Rites and Prayers," but the rites from Part I may be adapted.

49   Part III, "Texts from Sacred Scripture," includes the Scripture readings and psalms for the celebration of the funeral rites. Part IV, "Office for the Dead," includes "Morning Prayer," "Evening Prayer," and "Additional Hymns." Part V, "Additional Texts," contains "Prayers and Texts in Particular Circumstances" and "Holy Communion outside Mass." The texts that appear in the various rites in Parts I, II, and IV may be replaced by corresponding readings and psalms given in Part III and by corresponding prayers and texts given in Part V.

RITE OF COMMITTAL
FOR ADULTS

Joseph took Jesus down from the cross,
wrapped him in a shroud,
and laid him in a tomb

RITE OF COMMITTAL

204 The rite of committal, the conclusion of the funeral rites, is the final act of the community of faith in caring for the body of its deceased member. It may be celebrated at the grave, tomb, or crematorium and may be used for burial at sea. Whenever possible, the rite of committal is to be celebrated at the site of committal, that is, beside the open grave or place of interment, rather than at a cemetery chapel.

205 Two forms of the rite of committal are provided here: "Rite of Committal" and "Rite of Committal with Final Commendation." The first form is used when the final commendation is celebrated as part of the conclusion of the funeral liturgy. The second form is used when the final commendation does not take place during the funeral liturgy or when no funeral liturgy precedes the committal rite.

206 In committing the body to its resting place, the community expresses the hope that, with all those who have gone before marked with the sign of faith, the deceased awaits the glory of the resurrection. The rite of committal is an expression of the communion that exists between the Church on earth and the Church in heaven: the deceased passes with the farewell prayers of the community of believers into the welcoming company of those who need faith no longer but see God face to face.

STRUCTURE AND CONTENT
OF THE RITE OF COMMITTAL

207 Both forms of the committal rite begin with an invitation, Scripture verse, and a prayer over the place of committal. The several alternatives for the prayer over the place of committal take into account whether the grave, tomb, or resting place has already been blessed and situations in which the final disposition of the body will actually take place at a later time (for example, when the body is to be cremated or will remain in a cemetery chapel until burial at a later time).

208 The rite of committal continues with the words of committal, the intercessions, and the Lord's Prayer.

The rite of committal with final commendation continues with an invitation to prayer, a pause for silent prayer, the sprinkling and incensing of the body, where this is customary, the song of farewell, and the prayer of commendation (see nos. 227-231).

209 The act of committal takes place after the words of committal (in the rite of committal with final commendation, after the prayer of commen-

dation) or at the conclusion of the rite. The act of committal expresses the full significance of this rite. Through this act the community of faith proclaims that the grave or place of interment, once a sign of futility and despair, has been transformed by means of Christ's own death and resurrection into a sign of hope and promise.

210 Both forms of the rite conclude with a prayer over the people, which includes the verse *Eternal rest*, and a blessing. Depending on local custom, a song may then be sung and a gesture of final leave-taking may be made, for example, placing flowers or soil on the coffin.

ADAPTATION

211 If there is pastoral need for a longer committal rite than those provided here, for example, when the funeral liturgy has been celebrated on a previous day or in a different community, the minister may use the appropriate form of the committal rite and adapt it, for example, by adding a greeting, song, one or more readings, a psalm, and a brief homily. When there has been no funeral liturgy prior to the committal rite, the "Rite of Committal with Final Commendation" may be used and similarly adapted.

212 The rite of committal may be celebrated in circumstances in which the final disposition of the body will not take place for some time, for example, when winter delays burial or when ashes are to be interred at some time after cremation. The rite of committal may then be repeated on the later occasion when the actual burial or interment takes place. On the second occasion the rite may include a longer Scripture reading as well as a homily.

In the case of a body donated to science, the rite of committal may be celebrated whenever interment takes place.

MINISTRY AND PARTICIPATION

213 The community continues to show its concern for the mourners by participating in the rite of committal. The rite marks the separation in this life of the mourners from the deceased, and through it the community assists them as they complete their care for the deceased and lay the body to rest. The act of committal is a stark and powerful expression of this separation. When carried out in the midst of the community of faith, the committal can help the mourners to face the end of one relationship with the deceased and to begin a new one based on prayerful remembrance, gratitude, and the hope of resurrection and reunion.

By their presence and prayer members of the community signify their intention to continue to support the mourners in the time following the funeral.

214 The singing of well-chosen music at the rite of committal can help the mourners as they face the reality of the separation. At the rite of committal with final commendation, whenever possible, the song of farewell should be sung. In either form of the committal rite, a hymn or liturgical song that affirms hope in God's mercy and in the resurrection of the dead is desirable at the conclusion of the rite.

215 In the absence of a parish minister, a friend or member of the family should lead those present in the rite of committal.

The minister should vest according to local custom.

4 prayer P. 81 #37

4a) Song Farewell

OUTLINE OF THE RITE

Invitation
Scripture Verse
Prayer over the Place of Committal

Committal
Intercessions
The Lord's Prayer
Concluding Prayer

Prayer over the People

RITE OF COMMITTAL

INVITATION

> 216 When the funeral procession arrives at the place of committal, the minister says the following or a similar invitation.

Our brother/sister N. has gone to his/her rest in the peace of Christ. May the Lord now welcome him/her to the table of God's children in heaven. With faith and hope in eternal life, let us assist him/her with our prayers.

Let us pray to the Lord also for ourselves. May we who mourn be reunited one day with our brother/sister; together may we meet Christ Jesus when he who is our life appears in glory.

SCRIPTURE VERSE

> 217 One of the following verses or another brief Scripture verse is read. The minister first says:

We read in sacred Scripture: *P. 110*

A   Matthew 25:34   119

Come, you who are blessed by my Father, says the Lord,
inherit the kingdom prepared for you from the foundation
 of the world.

B   John 6:39   121

This is the will of the one who sent me, says the Lord,
that I should not lose anything of what he gave me,
but that I should raise it on the last day.

C   Philippians 3:20   124

Our citizenship is in heaven,
and from it we also await a savior,
the Lord Jesus Christ.

D   Revelation 1:5-6   126

Jesus Christ is the firstborn of the dead;
to him be glory and power forever and ever. Amen.

PRAYER OVER THE PLACE OF COMMITTAL

218 The minister says one of the following prayers or one of those provided in no. 405, p. 96.

A   If the place of committal is to be blessed:

Lord Jesus Christ,
by your own three days in the tomb,
you hallowed the graves of all who believe in you
and so made the grave a sign of hope
that promises resurrection
even as it claims our mortal bodies.

Grant that our brother/sister may sleep here in peace
until you awaken him/her to glory,
for you are the resurrection and the life.
Then he/she will see you face to face
and in your light will see light
and know the splendor of God,
for you live and reign for ever and ever.

R. Amen.

B   If the place of committal has already been blessed:

All praise to you, Lord of all creation.
Praise to you, holy and living God.
We praise and bless you for your mercy,
we praise and bless you for your kindness.
Blessed is the Lord, our God.

R. Blessed is the Lord, our God.

You sanctify the homes of the living
and make holy the places of the dead.
You alone open the gates of righteousness
and lead us to the dwellings of the saints.
Blessed is the Lord, our God.

R. Blessed is the Lord, our God.

We praise you, our refuge and strength.
We bless you, our God and Redeemer.
Your praise is always in our hearts and on our lips.
We remember the mighty deeds of the covenant.
Blessed is the Lord, our God.

R. Blessed is the Lord, our God.

Almighty and ever-living God,
remember the mercy with which you graced your servant N.
    in life.
Receive him/her, we pray, into the mansions of the saints.
As we make ready our brother's/sister's resting place,
look also with favor on those who mourn
and comfort them in their loss.

Grant this through Christ our Lord.

R. Amen.

C   When the final disposition of the body is to take place at a later
     time:

Almighty and ever-living God,
in you we place our trust and hope,
in you the dead, whose bodies were temples of the Spirit,
    find everlasting peace.

As we take leave of our brother/sister,
give our hearts peace in the firm hope
that one day N. will live
in the mansion you have prepared for him/her in heaven.

We ask this through Christ our Lord.

R. Amen.

COMMITTAL

219 The minister then says the words of committal. One of the
following formularies or one provided in no. 406, p. 98, may be
used.

A   Because God has chosen to call our brother/sister N.   55
     from this life to himself,
we commit his/her body to the earth
     [or the deep or the elements or its resting place],
for we are dust and unto dust we shall return.

But the Lord Jesus Christ will change our mortal bodies
     to be like his in glory,
for he is risen, the firstborn from the dead.

So let us commend our brother/sister to the Lord,
that the Lord may embrace him/her in peace
and raise up his/her body on the last day.

B In sure and certain hope of the resurrection to eternal life
   through our Lord Jesus Christ,
we commend to Almighty God our brother/sister N.,
and we commit his/her body to the ground
   [*or* the deep *or* the elements *or* its resting place]:
earth to earth, ashes to ashes, dust to dust.

The Lord bless him/her and keep him/her,
the Lord make his face to shine upon him/her
   and be gracious to him/her,
the Lord lift up his countenance upon him/her
   and give him/her peace.

> The committal takes place at this time or at the conclusion of
> the rite.

Intercessions

> 220 One of the following intercessions or those given in no. 407,
> p. 100, may be used or adapted to the circumstances, or new
> intercessions may be composed.

A   The minister begins:

For our brother/sister, N., let us pray to our Lord Jesus Christ,
who said, "I am the resurrection and the life. Whoever believes
in me shall live even in death and whoever lives and believes
in me shall never die." 56
75

Assisting minister:

Lord, you consoled Martha and Mary in their distress; draw
near to us who mourn for N., and dry the tears of those who
weep.
We pray to the Lord:

R. Lord, have mercy.

Assisting minister:

You wept at the grave of Lazarus, your friend; comfort us in
our sorrow.
We pray to the Lord:

R. Lord, have mercy.

Assisting minister:

You raised the dead to life; give to our brother/sister eternal life.
We pray to the Lord:

R. Lord, have mercy.

Assisting minister:

You promised paradise to the repentant thief; bring N. to the joys of heaven.
We pray to the Lord:

R. Lord, have mercy.

Assisting minister:

Our brother/sister was washed in baptism and anointed with the Holy Spirit; give him/her fellowship with all your saints.
We pray to the Lord:

R. Lord, have mercy.

Assisting minister:

He/she was nourished with your body and blood; grant him/her a place at the table in your heavenly kingdom.
We pray to the Lord:

R. Lord, have mercy.

Assisting minister:

Comfort us in our sorrow at the death of N.; let our faith be our consolation, and eternal life our hope.
We pray to the Lord:

R. Lord, have mercy.

B   The minister begins:

Dear friends, in reverence let us pray to God, the source of all   202
mercies.

Assisting minister:

Gracious Lord, forgive the sins of those who have died in Christ.
Lord, in your mercy:

R. Hear our prayer.

Assisting minister:

Remember all the good they have done.
Lord, in your mercy:

R. Hear our prayer.

Assisting minister:

Welcome them into eternal life.
Lord, in your mercy:

R. Hear our prayer.

Assisting minister:

Let us pray for those who mourn.
Comfort them in their grief.
Lord, in your mercy:

R. Hear our prayer.

Assisting minister:

Lighten their sense of loss with your presence.
Lord, in your mercy:

R. Hear our prayer.

Assisting minister:

Increase their faith and strengthen their hope.
Lord, in your mercy:

R. Hear our prayer.

Assisting minister:

Let us pray also for ourselves on our pilgrimage through life.
Keep us faithful in your service.
Lord, in your mercy:

R. Hear our prayer.

Assisting minister:

Kindle in our hearts a longing for heaven.
Lord, in your mercy:

R. Hear our prayer.

THE LORD'S PRAYER

> 221 In the following or similar words, the minister invites those present to pray the Lord's Prayer.

With longing for the coming of God's kingdom, let us pray:

> All say:

Our Father . . .

[handwritten: p. 10 Hymn with gentle winds]

CONCLUDING PRAYER

> 222 The minister says one of the following prayers or one of those provided in no. 408, p. 102.

A   God of holiness and power,   56
accept our prayers on behalf of your servant N.;
do not count his/her deeds against him/her,
for in his/her heart he/she desired to do your will.
As his/her faith united him/her to your people on earth,
so may your mercy join him/her to the angels in heaven.

We ask this through Christ our Lord.

R. Amen.

B   Almighty God,   199
through the death of your Son on the cross
you destroyed our death;
through his rest in the tomb
you hallowed the graves of all who believe in you;
and through his rising again
you restored us to eternal life.

God of the living and the dead,
accept our prayers
for those who have died in Christ
and are buried with him in the hope of rising again.
Since they were true to your name on earth,
let them praise you for ever in the joy of heaven.

We ask this through Christ our Lord.

R. Amen.

PRAYER OVER THE PEOPLE

223 The assisting minister says:

Bow your heads and pray for God's blessing.

All pray silently. The minister, with hands outstretched, prays over the people:

Merciful Lord,
you know the anguish of the sorrowful,
you are attentive to the prayers of the humble.
Hear your people
who cry out to you in their need,
and strengthen their hope in your lasting goodness.
We ask this through Christ our Lord.

R. Amen.

The minister then says the following:

Eternal rest grant unto him/her, O Lord.

R. And let perpetual light shine upon him/her.

May he/she rest in peace.

R. Amen.

May his/her soul and the souls of all the faithful departed,
through the mercy of God, rest in peace.

R. Amen.

A   A minister who is a priest or deacon says:

May the peace of God,
which is beyond all understanding,
keep your hearts and minds
in the knowledge and love of God
and of his Son, our Lord Jesus Christ.

R. Amen.

May almighty God bless you,
the Father, and the Son, ✠ and the Holy Spirit.

R. Amen.

B   A lay minister invokes God's blessing and signs himself or herself with the sign of the cross, saying:

May the love of God and the peace of the Lord Jesus Christ
bless and console us
and gently wipe every tear from our eyes:
in the name of the Father,
and of the Son, and of the Holy Spirit.

R. Amen.

The minister then concludes:

Go in the peace of Christ.

R. Thanks be to God.

A song may conclude the rite. Where it is the custom, some sign
or gesture of leave-taking may be made.

OUTLINE OF THE RITE

Invitation
Scripture Verse
Prayer over the Place of Committal

Invitation to Prayer
Silence
[Signs of Farewell]
Song of Farewell
Prayer of Commendation
Committal

Prayer over the People

RITE OF COMMITTAL
WITH FINAL COMMENDATION

INVITATION

> 224 When the funeral procession arrives at the place of committal, the minister says one of the following or a similar invitation.

A   We gather here to commend our brother/sister N. to God our Father and to commit his/her body to the earth/elements. In the spirit of faith in the resurrection of Jesus Christ from the dead, let us [raise our voices in song and] offer our prayers for N.

B   As we gather to commend our brother/sister N. to God our Father and to commit his/her body to the earth/elements, let us express in [song and] prayer our common faith in the resurrection. As Jesus Christ was raised from the dead, we too are called to follow him through death to the glory where God will be all in all.

SCRIPTURE VERSE

> 225 One of the following verses or another brief Scripture verse is read. The minister first says:

We read in sacred Scripture:

A   Matthew 25:34   119

Come, you who are blessed by my Father, says the Lord, inherit the kingdom prepared for you from the foundation of the world.

B   John 6:39   121

This is the will of the one who sent me, says the Lord, that I should not lose anything of what he gave me, but that I should raise it on the last day.

Our citizenship is in heaven,
and from it we also await a savior,
the Lord Jesus Christ.

D   Revelation 1:5-6   126

Jesus Christ is the firstborn of the dead;
to him be glory and power forever and ever. Amen.

Prayer over the Place of Committal

226 The minister says one of the following prayers or one of those
provided in no. 405, p. 96.

A   If the place of committal is to be blessed: 53

Lord Jesus Christ,
by your own three days in the tomb,
you hallowed the graves of all who believe in you
and so made the grave a sign of hope
that promises resurrection
even as it claims our mortal bodies.

Grant that our brother/sister may sleep here in peace
until you awaken him/her to glory,
for you are the resurrection and the life.
Then he/she will see you face to face
and in your light will see light
and know the splendor of God,
for you live and reign for ever and ever.

R. Amen.

B   If the place of committal has already been blessed:

All praise to you, Lord of all creation.
Praise to you, holy and living God.
We praise and bless you for your mercy,
we praise and bless you for your kindness.
Blessed is the Lord, our God.

R. Blessed is the Lord, our God.

You sanctify the homes of the living
and make holy the places of the dead.
You alone open the gates of righteousness
and lead us to the dwellings of the saints.
Blessed is the Lord, our God.

R. Blessed is the Lord, our God.

We praise you, our refuge and strength.
We bless you, our God and Redeemer.
Your praise is always in our hearts and on our lips.
We remember the mighty deeds of the covenant.
Blessed is the Lord, our God.

R. Blessed is the Lord, our God.

Almighty and ever-living God,
remember the mercy with which you graced your servant N.
   in life.
Receive him/her, we pray, into the mansions of the saints.
As we make ready our brother's/sister's resting place,
look also with favor on those who mourn
and comfort them in their loss.

Grant this through Christ our Lord.

R. Amen.

C   When the final disposition of the body is to take place at a later
       time:

Almighty and ever-living God,
in you we place our trust and hope,
in you the dead, whose bodies were temples of the Spirit,
   find everlasting peace.

As we take leave of our brother/sister,
give our hearts peace in the firm hope
that one day N. will live
in the mansion you have prepared for him/her in heaven.

We ask this through Christ our Lord.

R. Amen.

INVITATION TO PRAYER

227 Using one of the following invitations, or one of those provided in no. 402, p. 91, or in similar words, the minister faces the people and begins the final commendation.

A   Before we go our separate ways, let us take leave of our brother/ 185
     sister. May our farewell express our affection for him/her; may
     it ease our sadness and strengthen our hope. One day we shall
     joyfully greet him/her again when the love of Christ, which con-
     quers all things, destroys even death itself.

B   Trusting in God, we have prayed together for N. and now we 186
     come to the last farewell. There is sadness in parting, but we
     take comfort in the hope that one day we shall see N. again
     and enjoy his/her friendship. Although this congregation will
     disperse in sorrow, the mercy of God will gather us together
     again in the joy of his kingdom. Therefore let us console one
     another in the faith of Jesus Christ.

SILENCE

228 All pray in silence.

SIGNS OF FAREWELL

229 The coffin may now be sprinkled with holy water and incensed, or this may take place during or after the song of farewell.

SONG OF FAREWELL

230 The song of farewell is then sung. The following or other
responsories chosen from no. 403, p. 92, may be used or some
other song may be sung.

Saints of God, come to his/her aid! 47
Hasten to meet him/her, angels of the Lord!

R. Receive his/her soul and present him/her to God the Most High.

May Christ, who called you, take you to himself;
may angels lead you to the bosom of Abraham. R.

Eternal rest grant unto him/her, O Lord,
and let perpetual light shine upon him/her. R.

PRAYER OF COMMENDATION

231 The minister then says one of the following prayers.

A   Into your hands, Father of mercies,   48
we commend our brother/sister N.   67
in the sure and certain hope
that, together with all who have died in Christ,
he/she will rise with him on the last day.

[We give you thanks for the blessings
which you bestowed upon N. in this life:
they are signs to us of your goodness
and of our fellowship with the saints in Christ.]

Merciful Lord,
turn toward us and listen to our prayers:
open the gates of paradise to your servant
and help us who remain
to comfort one another with assurances of faith,
until we all meet in Christ
and are with you and with our brother/sister for ever.

We ask this through Christ our Lord.

R. Amen.

B   To you, O Lord, we commend the soul of N. your servant;   192
in the sight of this world he/she is now dead;
in your sight may he/she live for ever.

Forgive whatever sins he/she committed through human
     weakness
and in your goodness grant him/her everlasting peace.

We ask this through Christ our Lord.

R. Amen.

COMMITTAL

232 The act of committal takes place at this time or at the conclusion of the rite.

PRAYER OVER THE PEOPLE

233 The assisting minister says:

Bow your heads and pray for God's blessing.

All pray silently. The minister, with hands extended, prays over the people:

Merciful Lord,
you know the anguish of the sorrowful,
you are attentive to the prayers of the humble.
Hear your people
who cry out to you in their need,
and strengthen their hope in your lasting goodness.
We ask this through Christ our Lord.

R. Amen.

The minister then says the following:

Eternal rest grant unto him/her, O Lord.

R. And let perpetual light shine upon him/her.

May he/she rest in peace.

R. Amen.

May his/her soul and the souls of all the faithful departed,
through the mercy of God, rest in peace.

R. Amen.

A   A minister who is a priest or deacon says:

May the peace of God,
which is beyond all understanding,
keep your hearts and minds
in the knowledge and love of God
and of his Son, our Lord Jesus Christ.

R. Amen.

May almighty God bless you,
the Father, and the Son, ✠ and the Holy Spirit.

R. Amen.

B   A lay minister invokes God's blessing and signs himself or herself with the sign of the cross, saying:

May the love of God and the peace of the Lord Jesus Christ
bless and console us
and gently wipe every tear from our eyes:
in the name of the Father,
and of the Son, and of the Holy Spirit.

R. Amen.

The minister then concludes:

Go in the peace of Christ.

R. Thanks be to God.

A song may conclude the rite. Where it is the custom, some sign
or gesture of leave-taking may be made.

RITE OF COMMITTAL
FOR CHILDREN

Let the little children come to me;
it is to such as these that the kingdom of God belongs

FUNERAL RITES
FOR CHILDREN

234 Part II of the *Order of Christian Funerals* provides rites that are used in the funerals of infants and young children, including those of early school age. It includes "Vigil for a Deceased Child," "Funeral Liturgy," and "Rite of Committal."

Part II does not contain "Related Rites and Prayers," nos. 98-127, which are brief rites for prayer with the family and friends before the funeral liturgy. The rites as they are presented in Part I are models and should be adapted by the minister to the circumstances of the funeral for a child.

235 The minister, in consultation with those concerned, chooses those rites that best correspond to the particular needs and customs of the mourners. In some instances, for example, the death of an infant, only the rite of committal and perhaps one of the forms of prayer with the family may be desirable.

236 In the celebration of the funeral of a child the Church offers worship to God, the author of life, commends the child to God's love, and prays for the consolation of the family and close friends.

237 Funeral rites may be celebrated for children whose parents intended them to be baptized but who died before baptism.[1] In these celebrations the Christian community entrusts the child to God's all-embracing love and finds strength in this love and in Jesus' affirmation that the kingdom of God belongs to little children (see Matthew 19:14).

238 In its pastoral ministry to the bereaved the Christian community is challenged in a particular way by the death of an infant or child. The bewilderment and pain that death causes can be overwhelming in this situation, especially for the parents and the brothers and sisters of the deceased child. The community seeks to offer support and consolation to the family during and after the time of the funeral rites.

239 Through prayer and words of comfort the minister and others can help the mourners to understand that their child has gone before them into the kingdom of the Lord and that one day they will all be reunited there in joy. The participation of the community in the funeral rites is a sign of the compassionate presence of Christ, who embraced little children, wept at the death of a friend, and endured the pain and separation of death

---

[1] In the general catechesis of the faithful, pastors and other ministers should explain that the celebration of the funeral rites for children who die before baptism is not intended to weaken the Church's teaching on the necessity of baptism.

in order to render it powerless over those he loves. Christ still sorrows with those who sorrow and longs with them for the fulfillment of the Father's plan in a new creation where tears and death will have no place.

240 The minister should invite members of the community to use their individual gifts in this ministry of consolation. Those who have lost children of their own may be able in a special way to help the family as they struggle to accept the death of the child.

241 Those involved in planning the funeral rites for a deceased child should take into account the age of the child, the circumstances of death, the grief of the family, and the needs and customs of those taking part in the rites. In choosing the texts and elements of celebration, the minister should bear in mind whether the child was baptized or died before baptism.

242 Special consideration should be given to any sisters, brothers, friends, or classmates of the deceased child who may be present at the funeral rites. Children will be better able to take part in the celebration if the various elements are planned and selected with them in mind: texts, readings, music, gesture, processions, silence. The minister may wish to offer brief remarks for the children's benefit at suitable points during the celebration.

If children will be present at the funeral rites, those with requisite ability should be asked to exercise some of the liturgical roles. During the funeral Mass, for example, children may serve as readers, acolytes, or musicians, or assist in the reading of the general intercessions and in the procession with the gifts. Depending upon the age and number of children taking part, adaptations recommended in the *Directory for Masses with Children* may be appropriate.

RITE OF COMMITTAL

316 The rite of committal, the conclusion of the funeral rites (see nos. 204-215), is celebrated at the grave, tomb, or crematorium and may be used for burial at sea.

Three forms of the rite of committal are provided for the funeral of a child: "Rite of Committal," "Rite of Committal with Final Commendation," and "Rite of Final Commendation for an Infant."

317 The rite of committal is used when the final commendation and farewell is celebrated within the funeral liturgy. The rite of committal with final commendation is used when the final commendation is not celebrated within the funeral liturgy.

When the funeral liturgy is celebrated on a day prior to the committal or in a different community, the minister may wish to adapt the rite of committal, for example, by adding a song, a greeting, one or more readings, a psalm, and a brief homily. When no funeral liturgy precedes the rite of committal, the rite of committal with final commendation is used and should be similarly adapted.

318 The "Rite of Final Commendation for an Infant" may be used in the case of a stillborn or a newborn infant who dies shortly after birth. This short rite of prayer with the parents is celebrated to give them comfort and to commend and entrust the infant to God. This rite is a model and the minister should adapt it to the circumstances. It may be used in the hospital or place of birth or at the time of the committal of the body.

OUTLINE OF THE RITE

Invitation
Scripture Verse
Prayer over the Place of Committal

Committal
Intercessions
The Lord's Prayer
Concluding Prayer

Prayer over the People

RITE OF COMMITTAL

INVITATION

> 319 When the funeral procession arrives at the place of committal, the minister says the following or a similar invitation.

The life which this child N. received from his/her parents is not destroyed by death. God has taken him/her into eternal life.

As we commit his/her body to the earth/elements, let us comfort each other in our sorrow with the assurance of our faith, that one day we will be reunited with N.

SCRIPTURE VERSE

> 320 One of the following verses or another brief Scripture verse is read. The minister first says:

We read in sacred Scripture:

A   Matthew 25:34   119

Come, you who are blessed by my Father, says the Lord,
inherit the kingdom prepared for you from the foundation
   of the world.

B   John 6:39   121

This is the will of the one who sent me, says the Lord,
that I should not lose anything of what he gave me,
but that I should raise it on the last day.

C   Philippians 3:20   124

Our citizenship is in heaven,
and from it we also await a savior,
the Lord Jesus Christ.

D   Revelation 1:5-6   126

Jesus Christ is the firstborn of the dead;
to him be glory and power forever and ever. Amen.

Prayer over the Place of Committal

321 The minister says one of the following prayers or one of those provided in no. 405, p. 96.

A   If the place of committal is to be blessed: 230

O God,
by whose mercy the faithful departed find rest,
bless this grave,
and send your holy angel to watch over it.

As we bury here the body of N.,
welcome him/her into your presence,
that he/she may rejoice in you with your saints for ever.

We ask this through Christ our Lord.

R. Amen.

B   If the place of committal has already been blessed:

All praise to you, Lord of all creation.
Praise to you, holy and living God.
We praise and bless you for your mercy,
we praise and bless you for your kindness.
Blessed is the Lord, our God.

R. Blessed is the Lord, our God.

You sanctify the homes of the living
and make holy the places of the dead.
You alone open the gates of righteousness
and lead us to the dwellings of the saints.
Blessed is the Lord, our God.

R. Blessed is the Lord, our God.

We praise you, our refuge and strength.
We bless you, our God and Redeemer.
Your praise is always in our hearts and on our lips.
We remember the mighty deeds of the covenant.
Blessed is the Lord, our God.

R. Blessed is the Lord, our God.

Almighty and ever-living God,
remember the love with which you graced your child N. ~~Son Son~~
  in life.
Receive him/her, we pray, into the mansions of the saints.
As we make ready this resting place,
look also with favor on those who mourn
and comfort them in their loss.

Grant this through Christ our Lord.

R. Amen.

C　　　When the final disposition of the body is to take place at a later
　　　time:

Almighty and ever-living God,
in you we place our trust and hope,
in you the dead, whose bodies were temples of the Spirit,
  find everlasting peace.

As we take leave of N.,
give our hearts peace in the firm hope
that one day he/she will live
in the mansion you have prepared for him/her in heaven.

We ask this through Christ our Lord.

R. Amen.

COMMITTAL

322 The minister then says the words of committal. One of the
following formularies or one provided in no. 406, p. 98, may be
used.

A　　　A baptized child

Into your hands, O merciful Savior, we commend N. _Son_
Acknowledge, we humbly beseech you,
a sheep of your own fold, a lamb of your own flock.
Receive him/her into the arms of your mercy,
into the blessed rest of everlasting peace,
and into the glorious company of the saints in light.

We ask this through Christ our Lord —

B   A child who died before baptism

Lord God,
ever caring and gentle,
we commit to your love this little one [N.],
who brought joy to our lives for so short a time.
Enfold him/her in eternal life.

We pray for his/her parents
who are saddened by the loss of their child [baby/infant].
Give them courage
and help them in their pain and grief.
May they all meet one day
in the joy and peace of your kingdom.
We ask this through Christ our Lord.

R. Amen.

> The committal takes place at this time or at the conclusion of the rite.

INTERCESSIONS

> 323 The following intercessions or those given in no. 407, p. 100, may be used or adapted to the circumstances, or new intercessions may be composed.

> The minister begins:

Dear friends, let us turn to the Lord, the God of hope and consolation, who calls us to everlasting glory in Christ Jesus.

> Assisting minister:

For N., that he/she may now enjoy the place prepared for him/her in your great love.
We pray to the Lord.

R. Lord, hear our prayer.

> Assisting minister:

For N.'s father and mother [brother(s) and sister(s)], that they may know our love and support in their grief.
We pray to the Lord.

R. Lord, hear our prayer.

Assisting minister:

For his/her friends [and teachers], that they may love one another as you have loved us.
We pray to the Lord.

R. Lord, hear our prayer.

Assisting minister:

For this community, that we may bear one another's burdens.
We pray to the Lord.

R. Lord, hear our prayer.

Assisting minister:

For all those who mourn their children, that they may be comforted.
We pray to the Lord.

R. Lord, hear our prayer.

Assisting minister:

For all who are in need, that the fearful may find peace, the weary rest, and the oppressed freedom.
We pray to the Lord.

R. Lord, hear our prayer.

THE LORD'S PRAYER

324 Using the following or similar words, the minister invites those present to pray the Lord's Prayer.

As sons and daughters of a loving God, we pray in the confident words of his Son:

All say:

Our Father . . .

CONCLUDING PRAYER

325 The minister says one of the following prayers or one of those provided in no. 408, p. 102.

A   A baptized child

Tender Shepherd of the flock,
N. has entered your kingdom
and now lies cradled in your love.
Soothe the hearts of his/her parents
and bring peace to their lives.
Enlighten their faith
and give hope to their hearts.

Loving God,
grant mercy to your entire family in this time of suffering.
Comfort us in the knowledge that this child [N.]
lives with you and your Son, Jesus Christ,
and the Holy Spirit,
for ever and ever.

R. Amen.

B   A baptized child

Listen, O God, to the prayers of your Church
on behalf of the faithful departed,
and grant to your child, N.,
whose funeral we have celebrated today,
the inheritance promised to all your saints.

We ask this through Christ our Lord.

R. Amen.

C   A child who died before baptism

God of mercy,
in the mystery of your wisdom
you have drawn this child [N.] to yourself.
In the midst of our pain and sorrow,
we acknowledge you as Lord of the living and the dead
and we search for our peace in your will.
In these final moments we stand together in prayer,
believing in your compassion and generous love.
Deliver this child [N.] out of death
and grant him/her a place in your kingdom of peace.

We ask this through Christ our Lord.

R. Amen.

Prayer over the People

326 The assisting minister says:

Bow your heads and pray for God's blessing.

All pray silently. The minister, with hands outstretched, prays over the people:

Merciful Lord,
you know the anguish of the sorrowful,
you are attentive to the prayers of the humble.
Hear your people
who cry out to you in their need,
and strengthen their hope in your lasting goodness.
We ask this through Christ our Lord.

R. Amen.

The minister then says the following:

Eternal rest grant unto him/her, O Lord.

R. And let perpetual light shine upon him/her.

May he/she rest in peace.

R. Amen.

May his/her soul and the souls of all the faithful departed,
through the mercy of God, rest in peace.

R. Amen.

A   A minister who is a priest or deacon says:

May the peace of God,
which is beyond all understanding,
keep your hearts and minds
in the knowledge and love of God
and of his Son, our Lord Jesus Christ.

R. Amen.

May almighty God bless you,
the Father, and the Son, ✠ and the Holy Spirit.

R. Amen.

A lay minister invokes God's blessing and signs himself or herself with the sign of the cross, saying:

May the love of God and the peace of the Lord Jesus Christ
bless and console us
and gently wipe every tear from our eyes:
in the name of the Father,
and of the Son, and of the Holy Spirit.

R. Amen.

The minister then concludes:

Go in the peace of Christ.

R. Thanks be to God.

A song may conclude the rite. Where it is the custom, some sign or gesture of leave-taking may be made.

OUTLINE OF THE RITE

Invitation
Scripture Verse
Prayer over the Place of Committal

Invitation to Prayer
Silence
[Signs of Farewell]
Song of Farewell
Prayer of Commendation
Committal

Prayer over the People

RITE OF COMMITTAL
WITH FINAL COMMENDATION

INVITATION

327 When the funeral procession arrives at the place of committal, the minister says the following or a similar invitation.

The life which this child N. received from his/her parents is not destroyed by death. God has taken him/her into eternal life.

As we commend N. to God and commit his/her body to the earth/elements, let us express in [song and] prayer our common faith in the resurrection. As Jesus Christ was raised from the dead, we too are called to follow him through death to the glory where God will be all in all.

SCRIPTURE VERSE

328 One of the following verses or another brief Scripture verse is read. The minister first says:

We read in sacred Scripture:

A   Matthew 25:34   119

Come, you who are blessed by my Father, says the Lord, inherit the kingdom prepared for you from the foundation
    of the world.

B   John 6:39   121

This is the will of the one who sent me, says the Lord, that I should not lose anything of what he gave me, but that I should raise it on the last day.

C   Philippians 3:20   124

Our citizenship is in heaven, and from it we also await a savior, the Lord Jesus Christ.

D   Revelation 1:5-6   126

Jesus Christ is the firstborn of the dead; to him be glory and power forever and ever. Amen.

Prayer over the Place of Committal

329 The minister says one of the following prayers or one of those provided in no. 405, p. 96.

A If the place of committal is to be blessed:

O God,
by whose mercy the faithful departed find rest,
bless this grave,
and send your holy angel to watch over it.

As we bury here the body of N.,
welcome him/her into your presence,
that he/she may rejoice in you with your saints for ever.

We ask this through Christ our Lord.

R. Amen.

B If the place of committal has already been blessed:

All praise to you, Lord of all creation.
Praise to you, holy and living God.
We praise and bless you for your mercy,
we praise and bless you for your kindness.
Blessed is the Lord, our God.

R. Blessed is the Lord, our God.

You sanctify the homes of the living
and make holy the places of the dead.
You alone open the gates of righteousness
and lead us to the dwellings of the saints.
Blessed is the Lord, our God.

R. Blessed is the Lord, our God.

We praise you, our refuge and strength.
We bless you, our God and Redeemer.
Your praise is always in our hearts and on our lips.
We remember the mighty deeds of the covenant.
Blessed is the Lord, our God.

R. Blessed is the Lord, our God.

Almighty and ever-living God,
remember the love with which you graced your child N.
   in life.

Receive him/her, we pray, into the mansions of the saints.
As we make ready this resting place,
look also with favor on those who mourn
and comfort them in their loss.

Grant this through Christ our Lord.

R. Amen.

C   When the final disposition of the body is to take place at a later time:

Almighty and ever-living God,
in you we place our trust and hope,
in you the dead, whose bodies were temples of the Spirit,
   find everlasting peace.

As we take leave of N.,
give our hearts peace in the firm hope
that one day he/she will live
in the mansion you have prepared for him/her in heaven.

We ask this through Christ our Lord.

R. Amen.

Invitation to Prayer

330 Using one of the following invitations, or one of those provided in no. 402, p. 91, or in similar words, the minister faces the people and begins the final commendation.

A   A baptized child

God in his wisdom knows the span of our days; he has chosen to call to himself this child, whom he adopted as his own in baptism. The body we must now bury will one day rise again to a new and radiant life that will never end. 227

Our firm belief is that N., because he/she was baptized, has already entered this new life; our firm hope is that we shall do the same. Let us ask God to comfort his/her family and friends and to increase our desire for the joys of heaven.

B   A baptized child

With faith in Jesus Christ, we must reverently bury the body   228
of N.

Let us pray with confidence to God, in whose sight all creation
lives, that he will raise up in holiness and power the mortal body
of this [little] child, for God has chosen to number his/her soul
among the blessed.

C   A child who died before baptism

Let us commend this child to the Lord's merciful keeping; and   237
let us pray with all our hearts for N. and N. Even as they grieve
at the loss of their [little] child, they entrust him/her to the loving embrace of God.

Silence

331 All pray in silence.

Signs of Farewell

332 The coffin of a baptized child may now be sprinkled with
holy water and incensed, or this may take place during or after
the song of farewell.

Song of Farewell

333 The song of farewell is then sung. The following or other
responsories chosen from no. 403, p. 92, may be used or some
other song may be sung.

A   I know that my Redeemer lives: 189
on the last day I shall rise again.

R. And in my flesh I shall see God.

Or:

R. On the last day I shall rise again.

I shall see him myself, face to face;
and my own eyes shall behold my Savior. R.

Within my heart this hope I cherish:
that in my flesh I shall see God. R.

B   Saints of God, come to his/her aid!   47
Hasten to meet him/her, angels of the Lord!

R. Receive his/her soul and present him/her to God the
Most High.

May Christ, who called you, take you to himself;
may angels lead you to the bosom of Abraham. R.

Eternal rest grant unto him/her, O Lord,
and let perpetual light shine upon him/her. R.

PRAYER OF COMMENDATION

334 The minister then says one of the following prayers or one
of those provided in no. 404, p. 94.

A   A baptized child

You are the author and sustainer of our lives, O God.
You are our final home.
We commend to you N., our child.

In baptism he/she began his/her journey toward you.
Take him/her now to yourself
and give him/her the life
promised to those born again of water and the Spirit.

Turn also to us who have suffered this loss.
Strengthen the bonds of this family and our community.
Confirm us in faith, in hope, and in love,
so that we may bear your peace to one another
and one day stand together with all the saints
who praise you for your saving help.

We ask this in the name of your Son,
whom you raised from among the dead,
Jesus Christ, our Lord.

R. Amen.

B   A child who died before baptism

You are the author and sustainer of our lives, O God,
you are our final home.
We commend to you N., our child.

Trusting in your mercy
and in your all-embracing love,
we pray that you give him/her happiness for ever.

Turn also to us who have suffered this loss.
Strengthen the bonds of this family and our community.
Confirm us in faith, in hope, and in love,
so that we may bear your peace to one another
and one day stand together with all the saints
who praise you for your saving help.

We ask this in the name of your Son,
Jesus Christ, our Lord.

R. Amen.

COMMITTAL

335 The act of committal takes place at this time or at the conclusion of the rite.

PRAYER OVER THE PEOPLE

336 The assisting minister says:

Bow your heads and pray for God's blessing.

All pray silently. The minister, with hands extended, prays over the people:

Most merciful God,
whose wisdom is beyond our understanding,
surround the family of N. with your love,
that they may not be overwhelmed by their loss,
but have confidence in your goodness,
and strength to meet the days to come.

We ask this through Christ our Lord.

R. Amen.

The minister then says the following:

Eternal rest grant unto him/her, O Lord.

R. And let perpetual light shine upon him/her.

May he/she rest in peace.

R. Amen.

May his/her soul and the souls of all the faithful departed,
through the mercy of God, rest in peace.

R. Amen.

A   A minister who is a priest or deacon says:

May the peace of God,
which is beyond all understanding,
keep your hearts and minds
in the knowledge and love of God
and of his Son, our Lord Jesus Christ.

R. Amen.

May almighty God bless you,
the Father, and the Son, ✠ and the Holy Spirit.

R. Amen.

B   A lay minister invokes God's blessing and signs himself or herself with the sign of the cross, saying:

May the love of God and the peace of the Lord Jesus Christ
bless and console us
and gently wipe every tear from our eyes:
in the name of the Father,
and of the Son, and of the Holy Spirit.

R. Amen.

The minister then concludes:

Go in the peace of Christ.

R. Thanks be to God.

A song may conclude the rite. Where it is the custom, some sign
or gesture of leave-taking may be made.

OUTLINE OF THE RITE

Brief Address
Scripture Verse
Blessing of the Body
The Lord's Prayer
Prayer of Commendation
Blessing

RITE OF FINAL COMMENDATION
FOR AN INFANT

Brief Address

337 In the following or similar words, the minister addresses those who have assembled.

Dear friends, in the face of death all human wisdom fails. Yet the Lord Jesus teaches us, by the three days he spent in the tomb, that death has no hold over us. Christ has conquered death; his dying and rising have redeemed us. Even in our sorrow for the loss of this little child, we believe that, one short sleep past, he/she will wake eternally.

Scripture Verse

338 The minister then introduces the Scripture verse.

The Lord speaks to us now of our hope for this child in these words of consolation.

A member of the family or one of those present reads one of the following verses.

A   Romans 5:5b

The love of God has been poured out into our hearts through the holy Spirit that has been given to us.

B   1 John 3:2

Beloved, we are God's children now; what we shall be has not yet been revealed. We do know that when it is revealed we shall be like him, for we shall see him as he is.

Blessing of the Body

339 Using the following words, the minister blesses the body of
the deceased child.

Trusting in Jesus, the loving Savior,
who gathered children into his arms
and blessed the little ones,
we now commend this infant [N.]
  to that same embrace of love,
in the hope that he/she will rejoice
and be happy in the presence of Christ.

Then all join the minister, saying:

May the angels and saints lead him/her
to the place of light and peace
where one day
we will be brought together again.

The minister continues:

Lord Jesus,
lovingly receive this little child;
bless him/her
and take him/her to your Father.
We ask this in hope,
and we pray:

Lord, have mercy.

R. Lord, have mercy.

Christ, have mercy.

R. Christ, have mercy.

Lord, have mercy.

R. Lord, have mercy.

The Lord's Prayer

340 Using the following or similar words, the minister invites those present to pray the Lord's Prayer.

When Jesus gathered his disciples around him, he taught them to pray:

All say:

Our Father . . .

Prayer of Commendation

341 The minister then says the following prayer.

Tender Shepherd of the flock,
N. now lies cradled in your love.
Soothe the hearts of his/her parents
and bring peace to their lives.
Enlighten their faith
and give hope to their hearts.

Loving God,
grant mercy to your entire family in this time of suffering.
Comfort us with the hope that this child [N.]
lives with you and your Son, Jesus Christ,
and the Holy Spirit,
for ever and ever.

R. Amen.

Blessing

342 Using one of the following blessings, the minister blesses those present.

A   A minister who is a priest or deacon says:

May the God of all consolation
bring you comfort and peace,
in the name of the Father, ✠ and of the Son,
and of the Holy Spirit.

R. Amen.

B   A lay minister invokes God's blessing and signs himself or herself with the sign of the cross, saying:

May the God of all consolation
bring us comfort and peace,
in the name of the Father, and of the Son,
and of the Holy Spirit.

R. Amen.

ADDITIONAL TEXTS

The one who raised Christ Jesus from the dead
will give your mortal bodies
life through his Spirit living in you

PRAYERS AND TEXTS
IN PARTICULAR CIRCUMSTANCES

397 The following prayers for the dead and prayers for the mourners are for use in the various rites of Parts I, II, and IV.

The prayers are grouped as follows:

PRAYERS FOR THE DEAD (No. 398)

General, nos. 1-13
A pope, 14
A diocesan bishop, 15
Another bishop, 16
A priest, 17-19
A deacon, 20-21
A religious, 22-23
One who worked in the service of the Gospel, 24
A baptized child, 25-26
A young person, 27-28
Parents, 29
A parent, 30
A married couple, 31-33
A wife, 34
A husband, 35
A deceased non-Christian married to a Catholic, 36
An elderly person, 37-38
One who died after a long illness, 39-41
One who died suddenly, 42
One who died accidentally or violently, 43
One who died by suicide, 44-45
Several persons, 46-47

PRAYERS FOR THE MOURNERS (No. 399)

General, 1-7
A baptized child, 8-12
A child who died before baptism, 13-14
A stillborn child, 15

Prayers for the Dead

398 The following prayers for the dead may be used in the various rites of Parts I and II and in Part IV. The prayers should be chosen taking the character of the text into account as well as the place in the rite where it will occur. All of the prayers in this section end with the shorter conclusion. When a prayer is used as the opening prayer at the funeral liturgy, the longer conclusion is used.

1   General

God of faithfulness,   30
in your wisdom you have called your servant N.
  out of this world;
release him/her from the bonds of sin,
and welcome him/her into your presence,
so that he/she may enjoy eternal light and peace
and be raised up in glory with all your saints.

We ask this through Christ our Lord.

R. Amen.

2   General

Lord, in our grief we turn to you.   33
Are you not the God of love
who open your ears to all?

Listen to our prayers for your servant N.,
whom you have called out of this world:
lead him/her to your kingdom of light and peace
and count him/her among the saints in glory.

We ask this through Christ our Lord.

R. Amen.

3   General

Holy Lord, almighty and eternal God,   167
hear our prayers for your servant N.,
whom you have summoned out of this world.
Forgive his/her sins and failings
and grant him/her a place of refreshment, light,
  and peace.

Let him/her pass unharmed through the gates of death
to dwell with the blessed in light,
as you promised to Abraham and his children for ever.
Accept N. into your safekeeping
and on the great day of judgment
raise him/her up with all the saints
to inherit your eternal kingdom.

We ask this through Christ our Lord.

R. Amen.

4   General

Into your hands, O Lord,   168
we humbly entrust our brother/sister N.
In this life you embraced him/her with your tender love;
deliver him/her now from every evil
and bid him/her enter eternal rest.

The old order has passed away:
welcome him/her then into paradise,
where there will be no sorrow, no weeping nor pain,
but the fullness of peace and joy
with your Son and the Holy Spirit
for ever and ever.

R. Amen.

5   General

Almighty God and Father,   170
it is our certain faith
that your Son, who died on the cross, was raised from the dead,
the firstfruits of all who have fallen asleep.
Grant that through this mystery
your servant N., who has gone to his/her rest in Christ,
may share in the joy of his resurrection.

We ask this through Christ our Lord.

R. Amen.

6   General   171

O God,
glory of believers and life of the just,
by the death and resurrection of your Son, we are redeemed:
have mercy on your servant N.,
and make him/her worthy to share the joys of paradise,
for he/she believed in the resurrection of the dead.

We ask this through Christ our Lord.

R. Amen.

7   General   172

Almighty God and Father,
by the mystery of the cross, you have made us strong;
by the sacrament of the resurrection
you have sealed us as your own.
Look kindly upon your servant N.,
now freed from the bonds of mortality,
and count him/her among your saints in heaven.

We ask this through Christ our Lord.

R. Amen.

8   General   173

God of loving kindness,
listen favorably to our prayers:
strengthen our belief that your Son has risen from the dead
and our hope that your servant N. will also rise again.

We ask this through Christ our Lord.

R. Amen.

9   General   174

To you, O God, the dead do not die,
and in death our life is changed, not ended.
Hear our prayers
and command the soul of your servant N.
to dwell with Abraham, your friend,
and be raised at last on the great day of judgment.

In your mercy cleanse him/her of any sin
which he/she may have committed through human frailty.

We ask this through Christ our Lord.

R. Amen.

10   General

Lord God, in whom all find refuge,   175
we appeal to your boundless mercy:
grant to the soul of your servant N.
a kindly welcome,
cleansing of sin,
release from the chains of death,
and entry into everlasting life.

We ask this through Christ our Lord.

R. Amen.

11   General

God of all consolation,   176
open our hearts to your word,
so that, listening to it, we may comfort one another,
finding light in time of darkness
and faith in time of doubt.

We ask this through Christ our Lord.

R. Amen.

12   General

O God,
to whom mercy and forgiveness belong,
hear our prayers on behalf of your servant N.,
whom you have called out of this world;
and because he/she put his/her hope and trust in you,
command that he/she be carried safely home to heaven
and come to enjoy your eternal reward.

We ask this through Christ our Lord.

R. Amen.

13   General

O God,
in whom sinners find mercy and the saints find joy,
we pray to you for our brother/sister N.,
whose body we honor with Christian burial,
that he/she may be delivered from the bonds of death.
Admit him/her to the joyful company of your saints
and raise him/her on the last day
to rejoice in your presence for ever.

We ask this through Christ our Lord.

R. Amen.

14   A pope

O God,
from whom the just receive an unfailing reward,
grant that your servant N., our Pope,
whom you made vicar of Peter and shepherd of your Church,
may rejoice for ever in the vision of your glory,
for he was a faithful steward here on earth
of the mysteries of your forgiveness and grace.

We ask this through Christ our Lord.

R. Amen.

15   A diocesan bishop

Almighty and merciful God,
eternal Shepherd of your people,
listen to our prayers
and grant that your servant, N., our bishop,
to whom you entrusted the care of this Church,
may enter the joy of his eternal Master,
there to receive the rich reward of his labors.

We ask this through Christ our Lord.

R. Amen.

16   Another bishop

O God,
from the ranks of your priests
you chose your servant N.
to fulfill the office of bishop.

Grant that he may share
in the eternal fellowship of those priests
who, faithful to the teachings of the apostles,
dwell in your heavenly kingdom.

We ask this through Christ our Lord.

R. Amen.

17   A priest

God of mercy and love,
grant to N., your servant and priest,
a glorious place at your heavenly table,
for you made him here on earth
a faithful minister of your word and sacrament.

We ask this through Christ our Lord.

R. Amen.

18   A priest

O God,
listen favorably to our prayers
offered on behalf of your servant and priest,
and grant that N.,
who committed himself zealously to the service of your name,
may rejoice for ever in the company of your saints.

We ask this through Christ our Lord.

R. Amen.

19   A priest

Lord God,
you chose our brother N. to serve your people as a priest
and to share the joys and burdens of their lives.

Look with mercy on him
and give him the reward of his labors,
the fullness of life promised to those who preach your
    holy Gospel.

We ask this through Christ our Lord.

R. Amen.

20   *A deacon*

God of mercy,
as once you chose seven men of honest repute
to serve your Church,
so also you chose N. as your servant and deacon.
Grant that he may rejoice in your eternal fellowship
with all the heralds of your Gospel,
for he was untiring in his ministry here on earth.

We ask this through Christ our Lord.

R. Amen.

21   *A deacon*

Lord God,
you sent your Son into the world
to preach the Good News of salvation
and to pour out his Spirit of grace upon your Church.

Look with kindness on your servant N.
As a deacon in the Church
he was strengthened by the gift of the Spirit
to preach the Good News,
to minister in your assembly,
and to do the works of charity.

Give him the reward promised
to those who show their love of you
by service to their neighbor.

We ask this through Christ our Lord.

R. Amen.

22   *A religious*

All-powerful God,
we pray for our brother/sister N.,
who responded to the call of Christ
and pursued wholeheartedly the ways of perfect love.
Grant that he/she may rejoice
on that day when your glory will be revealed
and in company with all his/her brothers and sisters
share for ever the happiness of your kingdom.

We ask this through Christ our Lord.

R. Amen.

23   A religious

God of blessings,
source of all holiness,
the voice of your Spirit has drawn countless men and women
to follow Jesus Christ
and to bind themselves to you
with ready will and loving heart.

Look with mercy on N.
who sought to fulfill his/her vows to you,
and grant him/her the reward promised to all good and
    faithful servants.

May he/she rejoice in the company of the saints
and with them praise you for ever.

We ask this through Christ our Lord.

R. Amen.

24   One who worked in the service of the Gospel

Faithful God,   178
we humbly ask your mercy for your servant N.,
who worked so generously to spread the Good News:
grant him/her the reward of his/her labors
and bring him/her safely to your promised land.

We ask this through Christ our Lord.

R. Amen.

25   A baptized child

Lord, in our grief we call upon your mercy: 223
open your ears to our prayers,
and one day unite us again with N.,
who, we firmly trust,
already enjoys eternal life in your kingdom.

We ask this through Christ our Lord.

R. Amen.

26   A baptized child

To you, O Lord, 224
we humbly entrust this child,
so precious in your sight.
Take him/her into your arms
and welcome him/her into paradise,
where there will be no sorrow, no weeping nor pain,
but the fullness of peace and joy
with your Son and the Holy Spirit
for ever and ever.

R. Amen.

27   A young person

Lord, 177
your wisdom governs the length of our days.
We mourn the loss of N.,
whose life has passed so quickly,
and we entrust him/her to your mercy.
Welcome him/her into your heavenly dwelling
and grant him/her the happiness of everlasting youth.

We ask this through Christ our Lord.

R. Amen.

28   A young person

Lord God,
source and destiny of our lives,
in your loving providence
you gave us N.
to grow in wisdom, age, and grace.
Now you have called him/her to yourself.

As we grieve the loss of one so young,
we seek to understand your purpose.

Draw him/her to yourself
and give him/her full stature in Christ.
May he/she stand with all the angels and saints,
who know your love and praise your saving will.

We ask this through Christ our Lord.

R. Amen.

29   Parents

Lord God, who commanded us to honor father and mother, 181
look kindly upon your servants N. and N.,
have mercy upon them
and let us see them again in eternal light.

We ask this through Christ our Lord.

R. Amen.

30   A parent

God of our ancestors in faith,
by the covenant made on Mount Sinai
you taught your people to strengthen the bonds of family
through faith, honor, and love.
Look kindly upon N.,
a father/mother who sought to bind his/her children to you.
Bring him/her one day to our heavenly home
where the saints dwell in blessedness and peace.

We ask this through Christ our Lord.

R. Amen.

31   A married couple

Lord God, whose covenant is everlasting, 182
have mercy upon the sins of your servants N. and N.;
as their love for each other united them on earth,
so let your love join them together in heaven.

We ask this through Christ our Lord.

R. Amen.

32   A married couple

Eternal Father,
in the beginning you established the love of man and woman
as a sign of creation.
Your own Son loves the Church as a spouse.
Grant mercy and peace to N. and N. who,
by their love for each other,
were signs of the creative love
which binds the Church to Christ.

We ask this in the name of Jesus the Lord.

R. Amen.

33   A married couple

Lord God,
giver of all that is true and lovely and gracious,
you created in marriage a sign of your covenant.
Look with mercy upon N. and N.
You blessed them in their companionship,
and in their joys and sorrows you bound them together.
Lead them into eternal peace,
and bring them to the table
where the saints feast together in your heavenly home.
We ask this through Christ our Lord.

R. Amen.

34   A wife

Eternal God,
you made the union of man and woman
a sign of the bond between Christ and the Church.

Grant mercy and peace to N.,
who was united in love with her husband.
May the care and devotion of her life on earth
find a lasting reward in heaven.
Look kindly on her husband and family/children
as now they turn to your compassion and love.
Strengthen their faith and lighten their loss.
We ask this through Christ our Lord.

R. Amen.

35   A husband

Eternal God,
you made the union of man and woman
a sign of the bond between Christ and the Church.

Grant mercy and peace to N.,
who was united in love with his wife.
May the care and devotion of his life on earth
find a lasting reward in heaven.
Look kindly on his wife and family/children
as now they turn to your compassion and love.
Strengthen their faith and lighten their loss.
We ask this through Christ our Lord.

R. Amen.

36   A deceased non-Christian married to a Catholic

Almighty and faithful Creator,
all things are of your making,
all people are shaped in your image.
We now entrust the soul of N. to your goodness.
In your infinite wisdom and power,
work in him/her your merciful purpose,
known to you alone from the beginning of time.
Console the hearts of those who love him/her
in the hope that all who trust in you
will find peace and rest in your kingdom.

We ask this in the name of Jesus the Lord.

R. Amen.

37   An elderly person

God of endless ages,
from one generation to the next
you have been our refuge and strength.
Before the mountains were born
or the earth came to be,
you are God.
Have mercy now on your servant N.
whose long life was spent in your service.
Give him/her a place in your kingdom,
where hope is firm for all who love
and rest is sure for all who serve.

We ask this through Christ our Lord.

R. Amen.

38   An elderly person

God of mercy,
look kindly on your servant N.
who has set down the burden of his/her years.
As he/she served you faithfully throughout his/her life,
may you give him/her the fullness of your peace and joy.
We give thanks for the long life of N.,
now caught up in your eternal love.
We make our prayer in the name of Jesus who is our risen Lord
now and for ever.

R. Amen.

39   One who died after a long illness

God of deliverance,
you called our brother/sister N.
to serve you in weakness and pain,
and gave him/her the grace of sharing the cross of your Son.
Reward his/her patience and forbearance,
and grant him/her the fullness of Christ's victory.

We ask this through Christ our Lord.

R. Amen.

40   One who died after a long illness

Most faithful God,
lively is the courage of those who hope in you.
Your servant N. suffered greatly
but placed his/her trust in your mercy.
Confident that the petition of those who mourn
pierces the clouds and finds an answer,
we beg you, give rest to N.
Do not remember his/her sins
but look upon his/her sufferings
and grant him/her refreshment, light, and peace.

We ask this through Christ our Lord.

R. Amen.

41   One who died after a long illness

O God,
you are water for our thirst
and manna in our desert.
We praise you for the life of N.
and bless your mercy
that has brought his/her suffering to an end.
Now we beg that same endless mercy
to raise him/her to new life.
Nourished by the food and drink of heaven,
may he/she rest for ever
in the joy of Christ our Lord.

R. Amen.

42   One who died suddenly

180

Lord,
as we mourn the sudden death of our brother/sister,
show us the immense power of your goodness
and strengthen our belief
that N. has entered into your presence.

We ask this through Christ our Lord.

R. Amen.

43   One who died accidentally or violently

Lord our God,
you are always faithful and quick to show mercy.
Our brother/sister N.
was suddenly [and violently] taken from us.
Come swiftly to his/her aid,
have mercy on him/her,
and comfort his/her family and friends
by the power and protection of the cross.

We ask this through Christ our Lord.

R. Amen.

44   One who died by suicide

God, lover of souls,
you hold dear what you have made
and spare all things, for they are yours.
Look gently on your servant N.,
and by the blood of the cross
forgive his/her sins and failings.

Remember the faith of those who mourn
and satisfy their longing for that day
when all will be made new again
in Christ, our risen Lord,
who lives and reigns with you for ever and ever.

R. Amen.

45   One who died by suicide

Almighty God and Father of all,
you strengthen us by the mystery of the cross
and with the sacrament of your Son's resurrection.
Have mercy on our brother/sister N.
Forgive all his/her sins and grant him/her peace.
May we who mourn this sudden death be comforted
    and consoled by your power and protection.

We ask this through Christ our Lord.

R. Amen.

46   Several persons

O Lord,
you gave new life to N. and N.
in the waters of baptism;
show mercy to them now,
and bring them to the happiness of life in your kingdom.

We ask this through Christ our Lord.

R. Amen.

47   Several persons

All-powerful God,
whose mercy is never withheld
from those who call upon you in hope,
look kindly on your servants N. and N.,
who departed this life confessing your name,
and number them among your saints for evermore.

We ask this through Christ our Lord.

R. Amen.

Prayers for the Mourners

399 The following prayers for the mourners may be used in the various rites of Parts I and II. The prayers should be chosen taking the character of the text into account as well as the place in the rite where it will occur.

1   General

Father of mercies and God of all consolation,   34
you pursue us with untiring love
and dispel the shadow of death
with the bright dawn of life.

[Comfort your family in their loss and sorrow.
Be our refuge and our strength, O Lord,
and lift us from the depths of grief
into the peace and light of your presence.]

Your Son, our Lord Jesus Christ,
by dying has destroyed our death,
and by rising, restored our life.
Enable us therefore to press on toward him,
so that, after our earthly course is run,
he may reunite us with those we love,
when every tear will be wiped away.

We ask this through Christ our Lord.

R. Amen.

2   General

Lord Jesus, our Redeemer,   169
you willingly gave yourself up to death,
so that all might be saved and pass from death to life.
We humbly ask you to comfort your servants in their grief
and to receive N. into the arms of your mercy.
You alone are the Holy One,
you are mercy itself;
by dying you unlocked the gates of life
   for those who believe in you.
Forgive N. his/her sins,
and grant him/her a place of happiness, light, and peace
in the kingdom of your glory for ever and ever.

R. Amen.

3   General

God, all-compassionate,
ruler of the living and the dead,
you know beforehand
those whose faithful lives reveal them as your own.
We pray for those who belong to this present world
and for those who have passed to the world to come:
grant them pardon for all their sins.
We ask you graciously to hear our prayer
through the intercession of all the saints
and for your mercy's sake.

For you are God, for ever and ever.

R. Amen.

4   General

Lord our God,
the death of our brother/sister N.
recalls our human condition
and the brevity of our lives on earth.
But for those who believe in your love
death is not the end,
nor does it destroy the bonds
that you forge in our lives.
We share the faith of your Son's disciples
and the hope of the children of God.
Bring the light of Christ's resurrection
to this time of testing and pain
as we pray for N. and for those who love him/her,
through Christ our Lord.

R. Amen.

5   General

Lord God,
you are attentive to the voice of our pleading.
Let us find in your Son
comfort in our sadness,
certainty in our doubt,
and courage to live through this hour.
Make our faith strong
through Christ our Lord.

R. Amen.

6   General

Lord,
N. is gone now from this earthly dwelling
and has left behind those who mourn his/her absence.
Grant that as we grieve for our brother/sister
we may hold his/her memory dear
and live in hope of the eternal kingdom
where you will bring us together again.

We ask this through Christ our Lord.

R. Amen.

7   General

Most merciful God,
whose wisdom is beyond our understanding,
surround the family of N. with your love,
that they may not be overwhelmed by their loss,
but have confidence in your goodness,
and strength to meet the days to come.

We ask this through Christ our Lord.

R. Amen.

8   A baptized child

Lord of all gentleness,   225
surround us with your care
and comfort us in our sorrow,
for we grieve at the loss of this [little] child.

As you washed N. in the waters of baptism
and welcomed him/her into the life of heaven,
so call us one day
to be united with him/her
and share for ever the joy of your kingdom.

We ask this through Christ our Lord.

R. Amen.

9   A baptized child

Eternal Father,
through the intercession of Mary,
who bore your Son and stood by the cross as he died,
grant to these parents in their grief
the assistance of her presence,
the comfort of her faith,
and the reward of her prayers.

We ask this through Christ our Lord.

R. Amen.

10   A baptized child

Lord God,
source and destiny of our lives,
in your loving providence
you gave us N.
to grow in wisdom, age, and grace.
Now you have called him/her to yourself.

We grieve over the loss of one so young
and struggle to understand your purpose.

Draw him/her to yourself
and give him/her full stature in Christ.
May he/she stand with all the angels and saints,
who know your love and praise your saving will.

We ask this through Jesus Christ, our Lord.

R. Amen.

11   A baptized child

Merciful Lord,
whose wisdom is beyond human understanding,
you adopted N. as your own in baptism
and have taken him/her to yourself
even as he/she stood on the threshold of life.
Listen to our prayers and extend to us your grace,
that one day we may share eternal life with N.,
for we firmly believe that he/she now rests with you.

We ask this through Christ our Lord.

R. Amen.

12   A baptized child

Lord God,
from whom human sadness is never hidden,
you know the burden of grief
that we feel at the loss of this child.

As we mourn his/her passing from this life,
comfort us with the knowledge
that N. lives now in your loving embrace.

We ask this through Christ our Lord.

R. Amen.

13   A child who died before baptism

O Lord, whose ways are beyond understanding,   235
listen to the prayers of your faithful people:
that those weighed down by grief
at the loss of this [little] child
may find reassurance in your infinite goodness.

We ask this through Christ our Lord.

R. Amen.

14   A child who died before baptism

God of all consolation,   236
searcher of mind and heart,
the faith of these parents [N. and N.] is known to you.

Comfort them with the knowledge
that the child for whom they grieve
is entrusted now to your loving care.

We ask this through Christ our Lord.

R. Amen.

15   A stillborn child

Lord God,
ever caring and gentle,
we commit to your love this little one,
quickened to life for so short a time.
Enfold him/her in eternal life.

We pray for his/her parents
who are saddened by the loss of their child.
Give them courage
and help them in their pain and grief.
May they all meet one day
in the joy and peace of your kingdom.

We ask this through Christ our Lord.

℟. Amen.

FINAL COMMENDATION AND FAREWELL

INVITATION TO PRAYER

> 402 The following are alternatives to the invitation to prayer.

1   With faith in Jesus Christ, we must reverently bury the body 46
65
of our brother/sister.

Let us pray with confidence to God, in whose sight all creation lives, that he will raise up in holiness and power the mortal body of our brother/sister and command his/her soul to be numbered among the blessed.

May God grant him/her a merciful judgment, deliverance from death, and pardon of sin. May Christ the Good Shepherd carry him/her home to be at peace with the Father. May he/she re-joice for ever in the presence of the eternal King and in the company of all the saints.

2   Our brother/sister N. has fallen asleep in Christ. Confident in 183
our hope of eternal life, let us commend him/her to the loving mercy of our Father and let our prayers go with him/her. He/she was adopted as God's son/daughter in baptism and was nourished at the table of the Lord; may he/she now inherit the promise of eternal life and take his/her place at the table of God's children in heaven.

Let us pray also on our own behalf, that we who now mourn and are saddened may one day go forth with our brother/sister to meet the Lord of life when he appears in glory.

3   Because God has chosen to call our brother/sister N. 184
      from this life to himself,
we commit his/her body to the earth,
for we are dust and unto dust we shall return.

But the Lord Jesus Christ will change our mortal bodies
      to be like his in glory,
for he is risen, the firstborn from the dead.

So let us commend our brother/sister to the Lord,
that the Lord may embrace him/her in peace
and raise up his/her body on the last day.

4   Before we go our separate ways, let us take leave of our brother/ 185
sister. May our farewell express our affection for him/her; may
it ease our sadness and strengthen our hope. One day we shall
joyfully greet him/her again when the love of Christ, which con-
quers all things, destroys even death itself.

5   Trusting in God, we have prayed together for N. and now we 186
come to the last farewell. There is sadness in parting, but we
take comfort in the hope that one day we shall see N. again
and enjoy his/her friendship. Although this congregation will
disperse in sorrow, the mercy of God will gather us together
again in the joy of his kingdom. Therefore let us console one
another in the faith of Jesus Christ.

SONG OF FAREWELL

403 The following may be used as alternatives for the song of
farewell. These responsories may also be used during the entrance
procession in the celebration of the funeral liturgy.

1   Saints of God, come to his/her aid! 47
Hasten to meet him/her, angels of the Lord! 66
R. Receive his/her soul and present him/her to God the
Most High.

May Christ, who called you, take you to himself;
may angels lead you to the bosom of Abraham. R.

Eternal rest grant unto him/her, O Lord,
and let perpetual light shine upon him/her. R.

2   Lord our God, receive your servant, 187
for whom you shed your blood.
R. Remember, Lord, that we are dust: like grass, like a
flower of the field.

Merciful Lord, I tremble before you,
ashamed of the things I have done. R.

3   You knew me, Lord, before I was born. 188
You shaped me into your image and likeness.
R. I breathe forth my spirit to you, my Creator.

Merciful Lord, I tremble before you:
I am ashamed of the things I have done;
do not condemn me when you come in judgment. R.

4 I know that my Redeemer lives: 189
on the last day I shall rise again.
R. And in my flesh I shall see God.
    Or:
R. On the last day I shall rise again.

I shall see him myself, face to face;
and my own eyes shall behold my Savior.

Within my heart this hope I cherish:
that in my flesh I shall see God. R.

5 I know that my Redeemer lives, 189
And on that final day of days,
His voice shall bid me rise again:
Unending joy, unceasing praise!

This hope I cherish in my heart:
To stand on earth, my flesh restored,
And, not a stranger but a friend,
Behold my Savior and my Lord.

6 Lazarus you raised, O Lord, from the decay of the tomb. 190
R. Grant your servant rest, a haven of pardon and peace.

Eternal rest, O Lord,
and your perpetual light. R.

7 You shattered the gates of bronze 191
and preached to the spirits in prison.
R. Deliver me, Lord, from the streets of darkness.

A light and a revelation
to those confined in darkness. R.

"Redeemer, you have come,"
they cried, the prisoners of silence. R.

Eternal rest, O Lord,
and your perpetual light. R.

Prayer of Commendation

404 The following prayers may be used as alternative forms of the prayer of commendation.

1 A baptized person

Into your hands, Father of mercies,
we commend our brother/sister N.
in the sure and certain hope
that, together with all who have died in Christ,
he/she will rise with him on the last day.

[We give you thanks for the blessings
which you bestowed upon N. in this life:
they are signs to us of your goodness
and of our fellowship with the saints in Christ.]

Merciful Lord,
turn toward us and listen to our prayers:
open the gates of paradise to your servant
and help us who remain
to comfort one another with assurances of faith,
until we all meet in Christ
and are with you and with our brother/sister for ever.

We ask this through Christ our Lord.

R. Amen.

2 A baptized child

Lord Jesus,
like a shepherd who gathers the lambs
to protect them from all harm,
you led N. to the waters of baptism
and shielded him/her in innocence.

Now carry this little one
on the path to your kingdom of light
where he/she will find happiness
and every tear will be wiped away.

To you be glory, now and for ever.

R. Amen.

3 A baptized child

Into your gentle keeping, O Lord,
we commend this child [N.].
Though our hearts are troubled,
we hope in your loving kindness.

By the sign of the cross
he/she was claimed for Christ,
and in the waters of baptism
he/she died with Christ to live in him for ever.

May the angels, our guardians,
lead N. now to paradise
where your saints will welcome him/her
and every tear will be wiped away.
There we shall join in songs of praise for ever.

We ask this through Christ our Lord.

R. Amen.

RITE OF COMMITTAL

Prayer over the Place of Committal

405 One of the following may be used to bless the tomb or grave.

1 Lord Jesus Christ, 71
by your own three days in the tomb,
you hallowed the graves of all who believe in you
and so made the grave a sign of hope
that promises resurrection
even as it claims our mortal bodies.

Grant that our brother/sister may sleep here in peace
until you awaken him/her to glory,
for you are the resurrection and the life.
Then he/she will see you face to face
and in your light will see light
and know the splendor of God,
for you live and reign for ever and ever.

R. Amen.

2 O God, 193
by whose mercy the faithful departed find rest,
bless this grave,
and send your holy angel to watch over it.

As we bury here the body of our brother/sister,
deliver his/her soul from every bond of sin,
that he/she may rejoice in you with your saints for ever.

We ask this through Christ our Lord.

R. Amen.

3   Almighty God,
     you created the earth and shaped the vault of heaven;
     you fixed the stars in their places.
     When we were caught in the snares of death
     you set us free through baptism;
     in obedience to your will
     our Lord Jesus Christ
     broke the fetters of hell and rose to life,
     bringing deliverance and resurrection
     to those who are his by faith.
     In your mercy look upon this grave,
     so that your servant may sleep here in peace;
     and on the day of judgment raise him/her up
     to dwell with your saints in paradise.

     We ask this through Christ our Lord.

     R. Amen.

4   God of endless ages,
     through disobedience to your law
     we fell from grace
     and death entered the world;
     but through the obedience and resurrection of your Son
     you revealed to us a new life.
     You granted Abraham, our father in faith,
     a burial place in the promised land;
     you prompted Joseph of Arimathea
     to offer his own tomb for the burial of the Lord.
     In a spirit of repentance
     we earnestly ask you
     to look upon this grave and bless it,
     so that, while we commit to the earth the body of your servant N.
     his/her soul may be taken into paradise.

     We ask this through Christ our Lord.

     R. Amen.

COMMITTAL

406 The following are alternative forms of the committal.

1　　General

Because God has chosen to call our brother/sister N.
   from this life to himself,
we commit his/her body to the earth
   [or the deep or the elements or its resting place],
for we are dust and unto dust we shall return.

55
72

But the Lord Jesus Christ will change our mortal bodies
   to be like his in glory,
for he is risen, the firstborn from the dead.

So let us commend our brother/sister to the Lord,
that the Lord may embrace him/her in peace
and raise up his/her body on the last day.

2　　General

In sure and certain hope of the resurrection to eternal life
   through our Lord Jesus Christ,
we commend to Almighty God
   our brother/sister N. [N., our child],
and we commit his/her body to the ground
   [or the deep or the elements or its resting place]:
earth to earth, ashes to ashes, dust to dust.

The Lord bless him/her and keep him/her,
the Lord make his face to shine upon him/her
   and be gracious to him/her,
the Lord lift up his countenance upon him/her
   and give him/her peace.

3　　For ashes

My friends,
as we prepare to bury [entomb]
   the ashes of our brother/sister,
we recall that our bodies bear the imprint of the first creation
   when they were fashioned from dust;

but in faith we remember, too, that by the new creation
    we also bear the image of Jesus who was raised to glory.

In confident hope that one day God will raise us and transform
our mortal bodies, let us pray.

Pause for silent prayer.

Faithful God, *Ac*
Lord of all creation,
you desire that nothing redeemed by your Son
will ever be lost,
and that the just will be raised up on the last day.

Comfort us today with the word of your promise
as we return the ashes of our brother/sister to the earth.

Grant N. a place of rest and peace
where the world of dust and ashes has no dominion.
Confirm us in our hope that he/she will be created anew
on the day when you will raise him/her up in glory
to live with you and all the saints
for ever and ever. *10 0*

R. Amen.

4   For burial at sea

Lord God,
by the power of your Word
you stilled the chaos of the primeval seas,
you made the raging waters of the Flood subside,
and calmed the storm on the sea of Galilee.
As we commit the body of our brother/sister N. to the deep,
grant him/her peace and tranquility
until that day when he/she and all who believe in you
will be raised to the glory of new life
promised in the waters of baptism.

We ask this through Christ our Lord.

R. Amen.

INTERCESSIONS

407 The following may be used as an alternative form of the intercessions.

1 For our brother/sister, N., let us pray to our Lord Jesus Christ, who said, "I am the resurrection and the life. Whoever believes in me shall live even in death and whoever lives and believes in me shall never die."

Lord, you consoled Martha and Mary in their distress; draw near to us who mourn for N., and dry the tears of those who weep.
We pray to the Lord.

R. Lord, have mercy.

You wept at the grave of Lazarus, your friend; comfort us in our sorrow.
We pray to the Lord.

R. Lord, have mercy.

You raised the dead to life; give to our brother/sister eternal life.
We pray to the Lord.

R. Lord, have mercy.

You promised paradise to the repentant thief; bring N. to the joys of heaven.
We pray to the Lord:

R. Lord, have mercy.

Our brother/sister was washed in baptism and anointed with the Holy Spirit; give him/her fellowship with all your saints.
We pray to the Lord.

R. Lord, have mercy.

He/she was nourished with your body and blood; grant him/her a place at the table in your heavenly kingdom.
We pray to the Lord.

R. Lord, have mercy.

Comfort us in our sorrow at the death of N.; let our faith be our consolation, and eternal life our hope.
We pray to the Lord.

R. Lord, have mercy.

God of holiness and power,
accept our prayers on behalf of your servant N.;
do not count his/her deeds against him/her,
for in his/her heart he/she desired to do your will.
As his/her faith united him/her to your people on earth,
so may your mercy join him/her to the angels in heaven.

We ask this through Christ our Lord.

R. Amen.

2   Dear friends, our Lord comes to raise the dead and comforts
    us with the solace of his love. Let us praise the Lord Jesus Christ.

Word of God, Creator of the earth to which N. now returns:
in baptism you called him/her to eternal life to praise your
Father for ever:
Lord, have mercy.

R. Lord, have mercy.

Son of God, you raise up the just and clothe them with the glory
of your kingdom:
Lord, have mercy.

R. Lord, have mercy.

Crucified Lord, you protect the soul of N. by the power of your
cross, and on the day of your coming you will show mercy to
all the faithful departed:
Lord, have mercy.

R. Lord, have mercy.

Judge of the living and the dead, at your voice the tombs will
open and all the just who sleep in your peace will rise and sing
the glory of God:
Lord, have mercy.

R. Lord, have mercy.

All praise to you, Jesus our Savior, death is in your hands and
all the living depend on you alone:
Lord, have mercy.

R. Lord, have mercy.

Concluding Prayer

408 One of the following may be used as an alternative to the concluding prayer.

1   Listen, O God, to the prayers of your Church   196
on behalf of the faithful departed,
and grant to your servant N.,
whose funeral we have celebrated today,
the inheritance promised to all your saints.

We ask this through Christ our Lord.

R. Amen.

2   Loving God, from whom all life proceeds   197
and by whose hand the dead are raised again,
though we are sinners, you wish always to hear us.
Accept the prayers we offer in sadness for your servant N.:
deliver his/her soul from death,
number him/her among your saints
and clothe him/her with the robe of salvation
to enjoy for ever the delights of your kingdom.

We ask this through Christ our Lord.

R. Amen.

3   Lord God,   198
whose days are without end
and whose mercies beyond counting,
keep us mindful
that life is short and the hour of death unknown.
Let your Spirit guide our days on earth
in the ways of holiness and justice,
that we may serve you
in union with the whole Church,
sure in faith, strong in hope, perfected in love.
And when our earthly journey is ended,
lead us rejoicing into your kingdom,
where you live for ever and ever.

R. Amen.

SELECTED TEXTS
OF SACRED SCRIPTURE

We shall not live on bread alone,
but on every word that comes from God

OLD TESTAMENT READINGS

1   A reading from the book of Job   19:1, 23-27   83

I know that my Redeemer lives.

Job answered and said:

Oh, would that my words were written down!
   Would that they were inscribed in a record:
That with an iron chisel and with lead
   they were cut in the rock forever!
But as for me, I know that my Vindicator lives,
   and that he will at last stand forth upon the dust;
Whom I myself shall see:
   my own eyes, not another's, shall behold him,
And from my flesh I shall see God;
   my inmost being is consumed with longing.

This is the Word of the Lord.

2   A reading from the book of the prophet Isaiah   25:6a, 7-9   86

The Lord God will destroy death for ever.

On this mountain the Lord of hosts
   will provide for all peoples.
On this mountain he will destroy
   the veil that veils all peoples,
The web that is woven over all nations;
   he will destroy death forever.
The Lord God will wipe away
   the tears from all faces;
The reproach of his people he will remove
   from the whole earth; for the Lord has spoken.

On that day it will be said:
"Behold our God, to whom we looked to save us!
   This is the Lord for whom we looked;
   let us rejoice and be glad that he has saved us!"

This is the Word of the Lord.

A reading from the book of Lamentations   3:17-26

It is good to wait in silence for the Lord God to save.

My soul is deprived of peace,
   I have forgotten what happiness is;
I tell myself my future is lost,
   all that I hoped for from the Lord.

The thought of my homeless poverty
   is wormwood and gall;
Remembering it over and over
   leaves my soul downcast within me.
But I will call this to mind,
   as my reason to have hope:

The favors of the Lord are not exhausted,
   his mercies are not spent;
They are renewed each morning,
   so great is his faithfulness.
My portion is the Lord, says my soul;
   therefore will I hope in him.

Good is the Lord to one who waits for him,
   to the soul that seeks him;
It is good to hope in silence
   for the saving help of the Lord.

This is the Word of the Lord.

1   A reading from the letter of Paul to the Romans   6:3-4, 8-9 93

Let us walk in newness of life.

Are you unaware that we who were baptized into Christ Jesus were baptized into his death? We were indeed buried with him through baptism into death, so that, just as Christ was raised from the dead by the glory of the Father, we too might live in newness of life. If, then, we have died with Christ, we believe that we shall also live with him. We know that Christ, raised from the dead, dies no more; death no longer has power over him.

This is the Word of the Lord.

2   A reading from the letter of Paul to the Romans   8:14-23 94

We groan while we wait for the redemption of our bodies.

Those who are led by the Spirit of God are children of God. For you did not receive a spirit of slavery to fall back into fear, but you received a spirit of adoption, through which we cry, *"Abba, Father!"* The Spirit itself bears witness with our spirit that we are children of God, and if children, then heirs, heirs of God and joint heirs with Christ, if only we suffer with him so that we may also be glorified with him.

I consider that the sufferings of this present time are as nothing compared with the glory to be revealed for us. For creation awaits with eager expectation the revelation of the children of God; for creation was made subject to futility, not of its own accord but because of the one who subjected it, in hope that creation itself would be set free from slavery to corruption and share in the glorious freedom of the children of God. We know that all creation is groaning in labor pains even until now; and not only that, but we ourselves, who have the firstfruits of the Spirit, we also groan within ourselves as we wait for adoption, the redemption of our bodies.

This is the Word of the Lord.

3   A reading from the letter of Paul
    to the Romans   8:31b-35, 37-39

Who can ever come between us and the love of Christ?

If God is for us, who can be against us? He who did not spare
his own Son but handed him over for us all, how will he not also
give us everything else along with him? Who will bring a charge
against God's chosen ones? It is God who acquits us. Who will
condemn? It is Christ Jesus who died, rather, was raised, who
also is at the right hand of God, who indeed intercedes for us.

What will separate us from the love of Christ? Will anguish, or
distress, or persecution, or famine, or nakedness, or peril, or the
sword? No, in all these things we conquer overwhelmingly
through him who loved us. For I am convinced that neither death,
nor life, nor angels, nor principalities, nor present things, nor
future things, nor powers, nor height, nor depth, nor any other
creature will be able to separate us from the love of God in Christ
Jesus our Lord.

This is the Word of the Lord.

4   A reading from the letter of Paul
    to the Romans   14:7-9, 10b-12

Whether alive or dead, we belong to the Lord.

None of us lives for oneself, and no one dies for oneself. For if
we live, we live for the Lord, and if we die, we die for the Lord;
so then, whether we live or die, we are the Lord's. For this is
why Christ died and came to life, that he might be Lord of both
the dead and the living. For we shall all stand before the judgment seat of God; for it is written:

> "As I live, says the Lord, every knee shall bend before me,
> and every tongue shall give praise to God."

So then each of us shall give an account of himself to God.

This is the Word of the Lord.

5   A reading from the letter of Paul
to the Philippians   3:20-21   ₁₀₀

Jesus will transfigure these wretched bodies of ours to be like his glorious body.

Our citizenship is in heaven, and from it we also await a savior, the Lord Jesus Christ. He will change our lowly body to conform with his glorified body by the power that enables him also to bring all things into subjection to himself.

This is the Word of the Lord.

6   A reading from the book of Revelation   14:13   ₁₀₅

Happy are those who die in the Lord.

I heard a voice from heaven say, "Write this: Blessed are the dead who die in the Lord from now on." "Yes," said the Spirit, "let them find rest from their labors, for their works accompany them."

This is the Word of the Lord.

7   A reading from the book of Revelation   21:1-5a, 6b-7   ₁₀₇

There will be no more death.

I saw a new heaven and a new earth. The former heaven and the former earth had passed away, and the sea was no more. I also saw the holy city, a new Jerusalem, coming down out of heaven from God, prepared as a bride adorned for her husband. I heard a loud voice from the throne saying, "Behold, God's dwelling is with the human race. He will dwell with them and they will be his people and God himself will always be with them as their God. He will wipe every tear from their eyes, and there shall be no more death or mourning, wailing or pain, for the old order has passed away."

The one who sat on the throne said, "Behold, I make all things new. I am the Alpha and the Omega, the beginning and the end. To the thirsty I will give a gift from the spring of life-giving water. The victor will inherit these gifts, and I shall be his God, and he will be my son."

This is the Word of the Lord.

1   A reading from the holy gospel
    according to Matthew   11:25-30   129

Come to me . . . and I will give you rest.

On one occasion Jesus spoke thus: "I give praise to you, Father, Lord of heaven and earth, for although you have hidden these things from the wise and the learned you have revealed them to the childlike. Yes, Father, such has been your gracious will. All things have been handed over to me by my Father. No one knows the Son except the Father, and no one knows the Father except the Son and anyone to whom the Son wishes to reveal him.

"Come to me, all you who labor and are burdened, and I will give you rest. Take my yoke upon you and learn from me, for I am meek and humble of heart; and you will find rest for yourselves. For my yoke is easy, and my burden light."

This is the Gospel of the Lord.

2   A reading from the holy gospel
    according to Mark   10:13-16

The kingdom of heaven belongs to little children.

People were bringing children to Jesus that he might touch them, but the disciples rebuked them. When Jesus saw this he became indignant and said to them, "Let the children come to me; do not prevent them, for the kingdom of God belongs to such as these. Amen, I say to you, whoever does not accept the kingdom of God like a child will not enter it." Then he embraced them and blessed them, placing his hands on them.

This is the Gospel of the Lord.

3   A reading from the holy gospel
according to Luke   12:35-40   134

Be prepared.

Jesus said to his disciples:

"Gird your loins and light your lamps and be like servants who await their master's return from a wedding, ready to open immediately when he comes and knocks. Blessed are those servants whom the master finds vigilant on his arrival. Amen, I say to you, he will gird himself, have them recline at table, and proceed to wait on them. And should he come in the second or third watch and find them prepared in this way, blessed are those servants. Be sure of this: if the master of the house had known the hour when the thief was coming, he would not have let his house be broken into. You also must be prepared, for at an hour you do not expect, the Son of Man will come."

This is the Gospel of the Lord.

4   A reading from the holy gospel
according to John   12:23-26   142

If a grain of wheat falls on the ground and dies, it yields a rich harvest.

Jesus told his disciples:

"The hour has come for the Son of Man to be glorified. Amen, amen, I say to you, unless a grain of wheat falls to the ground and dies, it remains just a grain of wheat; but if it dies, it produces much fruit. Whoever loves his life loses it, and whoever hates his life in this world will preserve it for eternal life. Whoever serves me must follow me, and where I am, there also will my servant be. The Father will honor whoever serves me."

This is the Gospel of the Lord.